RHODESIAN BLACK BEHIND BARS

by

Didymus Mutasa

For Nate Patel, the son-
in-law. In remembarance,
of the good time spent with
the author at Rusape.

2/8/85

M

MOWBRAYS
LONDON & OXFORD

Set in 11/12 pt. IBM Press Roman, by Hope Services, Wantage and
printed and bound in Great Britain by Redwood Burn Limited,
Trowbridge and Esher.

ISBN 0264 660110 (paperback)
ISBN 0264 662318 (hardback)

First published in 1974 by A. R. Mowbray & Co. Ltd.,
The Alden Press, Osney Mead, Oxford, OX2 0EG

ERRATUM

Peter Niesewand's name is wrongly
spelt on pages iii and ix.

Contents

Dedication

This book is dedicated to my compatriots detained by the illegal regime in Zimbabwe (Rhodesia) in the prisons at Wha Wha, Gwelo, Salisbury, Buffalo Range, Que-Que, Sengwe (Gonakudzingwa), Marandellas, Chikirubi.

Thomas Zwenyika AFRICA, Langton Kufa BANDA, Kokoro Linbani BASIKORO, Lampkeni BAURENI, Manyika BAYDE, Pamganyi Mushonga Bulawa BEN, Ronald Augustus BENNET, Edward BHEBE, Robert S. BHEBHE, Tiki BURIRA, Tauzeni BUTAMUZUKA, Joe BOMBA, Jackson Francis CHADEREKA, Amon CHADOKA, Jairos CHADOKA, Arthur CHADZINGWA, Nyemba CHAGADAMA, CHAMPION, Chiyambata Tobias CHANIRO, Freddy CHAREKA, Zvite Saul CHAREKA, Nyson Julias CHARTSAMA, James Bernard CHATAGWE, Charles CHAWANDA, Dzawanda Robert CHICHETU, Enock CHIDAVAENZI, Josia Tsikayi CHIDAVAENZI, Kadonda Kanjunja CHIDODO, Aaron CHIGAZIRA, Poulos CHIGEDE, John CHIGODORA, Michael CHIHOPE, Rangton CHIHUMBIRI, Noël William CHIKANYA, Reuben CHIKWANHA, Ernest CHILIMANZI, Wisdom CHIMANGA, Chocho CHIMOMBE, Samuel Mutambo Simon CHIMOMBE, Peter CHIMUSUMBU, Emson CHINAKA, Josiah CHINAMANO, Mrs. Josiah CHINAMANO, Jefrey Tizora CHINEMBIRI, Janate CHINOGORO, Mairisi CHINONGORO, Rita CHINOGORO, Watson CHIOTA, Maylkotl CHIPAMURANDU, Shadreck CHIPANGA, Mr. CHIREMBWE, David CHIROMBO, Anton CHIRUME, Kenneth CHISANGO*, Desiderio CHISIMUKA, Cyril Chirire CHITONGO, Nyamandu CHITSENDE, Pedro CHITUWU, Samson Madade CHIUTSE, Wilfred CHIVAKO, Ferasi CHIWASHIRA, Raymond CHIWASHIRA, Elisha Nzirasha CIGUDU, Davi Ramiyosi CWERERA, Robert DAMBUDZO, Tema DAMSON, Phinias Marufu DANGA Jeremiah DUBE,

Fred Vincent DUBE, Mbambe DZAPASI, Kembo Solomon DZINAMURUNGU, Saineti DZINODAVIRA, Fridge ERIYA, Gujga FORGET, Emuwati FOYA, Phillimon GATSI, Charles GIBBS, Boniface GUMBO, Dick GUMBURA, Prince GUMEDE, Patrick Gufu GURUPIRA, John GUZHA, Adam GWERERA, Joseph GWIBA, Douglas Nhengu HODZA, Bishom HUMBASHA, Karikoga Kiva JAM, Zuse JONAS, Mutova Tayiroti KABIRO, Daniel KABIYA, Munetsi KADENHE, Willie KADENHE, John KADZUNGURA, Crispen KAFUMHE, Orfero KAGANDE, Amon Chibika KAHONDE, Norbert KAINGIDZA, Richard KAKUNGUWO, Dzabaya KAMBITI, Mr. KAMUTASHU, Joseph KAMWARAMWAZHA, Raymond KANDIYE, Simon KANHEMA, Zacharia KANYASA, Mr. KAPOSONORE, John KARUMBO, Chiriwa KASERE, Naison KATONJE, Peter Abraham KATSANDE, Nyamayagora KATSANDE, Jairosi KATSIGA, Rufaro John KAVIYI, George KAWENDA, Benjamin KAYENDA, Mr. KAZERENGA, Baidoni KESIYASI, Madiyane Lanford KESWA, Jefrety Bofana KHUMALO, Mazvimbakupa KIDO, Moses KUNAKA, Bamusi KUSENI, Reginald MABACHI, Hohannes Mandiundu Toso MABENA, Norman MABENA, Welsham MABENA, Oscar Dandauro MADZARANGANWA, Jackson MADZIKA, Daniel MADZIMBAMUTO, Kamundori MAGETSI, Zachariah MAGIDI, Bernard MAGWAZA, Gilbert MAJIRI, Meja MAKAMBA, Willie MAKARATI, Mishek MAKHENA, Changadzo MAKO, John Ruredzo MAKONI, Maman Michael MAKURA, John MAKWASHA, Moton Dizzi Paul MALIANGA, Sidney Donald MALUNGA, Ketero MANDAZA, Kinson MANDEBVU, Garikayi MANDIZHA, Lawrence MANGOMA, Lameck MANOTA, Lucas William MANYATELA, George MARANGE, Simon MAREMBO, Zira MARIFONDE, Mhere Shepherd MARINGE, Kadzungura MARITINYI, Kamusawu MARITINYI, Seda MARITINYI, Emmanuel MASANGO, Merek Naison MASAYI, John MASHAKADA, Miles MASHAYAMOMBE, Charles MASHONETA, Sahanya MASHONGA, Juta MASINA, Robinson MASUNDA, Jacob MATAPURETA, Isaac Chisaka MAWODZEKA, Switin MBAMBO, Walter Mbambo MBAMBO, Enos MBOFANA, Standford Mubay MFURA, Chiposira MHANDU, Tobias MHESA, Benoni Fote Isangu MHETE, Titus MHETU, Amos MKWAMANZI, Wilfred Tsampu MLALA, Pious MLILO, Mr. MOKIYATI, Canaan MOYO, Elliot Mapenduka MOYO, John Machosi MOYO, Neville MOYO, Vote Henry MOYO, Clark Mgiyo MPOFU, Major MPOFU, Pollant Jabavu MPOFU, Joseph MSIKA, Amos MSONGELWA, Elias Paulus MTSHIYA, John Tawona MTUVA, Tom MUBAYIRA, Clement

vi

MUCHACHI, Andrew MUCHENJE, Kowo MUDZAMISA, Robert
Gabriel MUGABE, Nevison MUKANGANGA; Linos MUKARO, Aaron
Deza MUKINI, Gotso MUNGAZE, George David MUNYORO,
Ghawonza Abel MURINGAZUVA, Willie MUSARURWA, Sami Katonje
MUSHAWOMHUKA, Edward MUSHAYADURA, Orbert Denga Enock
MUSHAYIRE, Nice MUSIWA, Jack MUSOKERI, Langton MUTAPE,
Paison MUTAUMA, Clarkson MUTEMA, Virimayi Jeremiah MUVIRINI
CHAMBA, Jowel MVURI, Adolphus MWANE, Chokupara NARITI,
Frank Chakarama NAVAYA, Tukamuka Adam NAVAYA, Michael
NCUBE, Mishek NCUBE, Richard NCUBE, Simon NCUBE, Lawrence
NDHLELA, Agrippa NDHLOVU, Douglas Majoli NDHLOVU, Joel
NDHLOVU, Moffat NDHLOVU, Naison NDHLOVU, Peter Madlela
NDHLOVU, Raphael NDHLOVU, Sikillele NDHLOVU, Alfred
NDHLUMBE, Augustine NEWET, Charlton NGCEBETSHA,
Mudzingwa NHAMHERE, Keyi NKAKA, Enas Muzombi NKALA,
Lazurus NKALA, Joshua NKOMO, Lovemore NOTICE, Elijah NOYO,
Morris NYAGUMBO, Ringi NYAGUZE, Fox NYAHUMA, Joseph
NYAKATANGURA, Jackson Mja NYAMAKOPE, Poki NYAMAPHEKA,
Kwirirayi NYAMUNZE, Smart PINDURA, Karuwe POULOS,
Chimupanga RAIMOSI, Tinopi Shadreck RAMBANAPASI, Zesi
RAYISON, Benjamin Chifani RUWISI, Chipfunde SAINETI, Midirosi
SAJENI, Christopher SAKALA, Ignatus Kadozvo SHADRECK,
Samson SHIRENI, Cephas SIBANDA, Mabelani Ngwenyama SIBANDA,
Peter SIBANDA, Gabriel SIKOTI, Pauline SIKOTI, Rudo SIKOTI,
Ndabaningi SITHOLE, Abel SIWELA, Moses Tusi Ndiweni TAIMON,
Mairosi TAPERERWA, Ben Kuda TAPUTSA, Jayirosi TARGWIREYI,
Edson TAURO, Edgar TEKERE, Johane TIKI, Garfield TODD, Aleck
TSHABANGU, Edward TSHUMA, Donanzi UNGWA, Wilson Kamwendo
URIRI, Xaverio VIRUKAYI, Mr. WILLIS, Kirimu Kamazeya WINDOW,
Kasina WISTON, John Clarence WYCILIFF, Raymond ZHARARE,
Mose ZHOYA, Norman ZIKALE, Thomas ZINGAYI, Kenneth Tione
ZUZE, Mashapure Fourpence ZWAUYA, Shame ZWIKARAMBA,
Stephen Joshua ZWINAVASHE MUSUNGWA.

*Kenneth Chisango died 15 January 1974.

Foreword

by Peter Neiswand

Didymus Mutasa was a very dangerous man in Ian Smith's Rhodesia, and it came as no surprise at all when he was arrested and placed in indefinite detention without trial or charge.

Mr Mutasa was an ungrateful trouble-maker. As Government officials pointed out he had received a good education and was a rising civil servant when he threw up everything to do social work. In a materialistic society this was a matter for surprise, and in some cases, suspicion.

White fears were soon justified. Mr Mutasa became the instigator and chairman of the Cold Comfort Farm Society, an extraordinary organisation in the Rhodesian context. In essence the Farm was a non-racial kibbutz on the outskirts of the capital; an oasis of integration in a country becoming increasingly committed to racialism.

Cold Comfort Farm was run on a co-operative basis by about 40 people, mostly Africans. They worked hard during the day, earning only 'pocket money' and studying or holding discussions during the evening. They were energetic and alert. Not surprisingly, perhaps, the members of Cold Comfort Farm were not active supporters of the Rhodesian Government but believed, that the 5·5 million black majority, were being given a raw deal by Europeans and should be given separate power. The most dangerous thing was the fact that the Farm and its members operated on a basic Christian principle sharing work and rewards and caring little for the luxuries which dominated the lives of the white society around them. The Rhodesian Government called it 'Communism'. Desmond Lardner-Burke, the Minister of Law & Order said the Society had cultivated 'an innocent image' but was in reality 'a centre of intrigue'. Cold Comfort Farm was declared a banned organisation, its members expelled, dispersed or arrested.

A few hours before the police moved in, one African member told me 'they can ban the Society and take away our land but Cold Comfort Farm is an idea and a way of life, and we will take it with us in our hearts wherever we go'.

The police raid came at dawn, as we expected they would and soon the Farm was clear of all the society's officials. A sign was posted outside declaring it to be a 'protected area'. Protected from whom?

1
Into Prison

Everisto, a young man who shared a bedroom together with my two sons at Cold Comfort Farm, woke up at five o'clock to prepare breakfast for himself and others going to school as usual. This time he found it necessary to come to our bedroom, and he knocked at our door. He told us that there were a lot of cars in the car park and many people waiting to see us. Immediately, the police knocked at the same bedroom door and announced themselves. They handed us a search warrant which indicated that they wanted to search around the house and look at everything that belonged to us. An African security policeman was instructed to follow me round the house and never be away from me. I asked them what they were looking for just in case I might be able to tell them and avoid wasting their time. They told me not to mind because they knew what they were looking for. A man was searching every room that belonged to us. We asked again what they were looking for and they replied that they were searching for bombs and guns. I said that they were looking for them in the wrong place. As this was happening to us, the same thing was happening to Guy and Molly Clutton-Brock and to the people who

1

lived in the cottages down below.

The search lasted about four hours. We were hungry, so Gertrude prepared some coffee and offered some to the security men who were very surprised at her hospitality. We asked them to invite in the other policemen who were standing outside guarding the house, and those who came asked 'Is this the room where the coffee is being served?'. Gertrude, smiling, served them all as hospitably as she could. At the end of the search we all assembled at the farmhouse and began to tell one another our experiences during the search. At the same time the police were collecting together those of our belongings which they wanted to take away, and getting us to sign for them. While this was going on most of the policemen departed and went back to Salisbury. However, the African policeman who had been instructed to follow me continued to do so, and I was a little bit surprised because I expected him to go back with the rest of the police. A little later, one of the white security policemen, Mr Chalk, came to me and asked me to go to the next room with him. I followed him there and he handed me the following order, detaining me to Sinoia Prison. It reads:

ORDER IN TERMS OF SECTION 16 OF THE
EMERGENCY POWERS (MAINTENANCE OF LAW AND ORDER)
REGULATIONS, 1970.

To: Didymus Noel Edwin Mutasa (X24783 Makoni)

You are hereby notified that it appears to me that it is expedient in the interests of public safety or public order to make an Order against you in terms of subsection (1) of section 16 of the Emergency Powers (Maintenance of Law and Order) Regulations, 1970.

2

2 The making of this Order is based on a belief that you are likely to commit, or to incite the commission of, acts in Rhodesia which would endanger the public safety, or disturb or interfere with the maintenance of public order.

3 Now, Therefore, in terms of subsection (1) of section 16 of the Emergency Powers (Maintenance of Law and Order) Regulations, 1970, I do hereby order that you shall be detained by being kept in the place described in the Schedule to this Order until the revocation or expiry of the Declaration of a Public Emergency in Rhodesia or until this Order is revoked or varied.

4 Under the provisions of subsection (1) of section 50 of the aforesaid Regulations, this Order shall come into force immediately it is delivered or tendered to you, but you have the right to object and to make representations in writing to me within seven days after the Order has been delivered or tendered to you stating the reason or reasons why you consider that the Order should be revoked.

5 In addition, you are advised that, in terms of subsection (1) of section 30 of the aforesaid Regulations, you may at any time within three months beginning on the date on which your detention was ordered, apply in writing to me for your case to be reviewed by the Review Tribunal established by section 25 of the aforesaid Regulations, and in any such application you should state the reasons why you consider that the detention order should be reviewed.

Given under my hand at Salisbury this 13th day of November, 1970.

D. W. Lardner-Burke
MINISTER OF LAW AND ORDER

After reading the order, I went back into the room where the rest of the people were and broke the news of my detention to them and handed my detention order to Guy. Holding it, he said to the security policeman,

'This is an illegal document made by an illegal regime who unlawfully seized power in this country. It has no legal standing whatsoever. Whilst the guns and control of force in this country are in the hands of this illegal regime there is nothing we can do although to the rest of the world this document has no standing. I will do my part. I shall let everyone know. We have to tell it to the world. This won't concern me because I shall be gone, but I feel sorry for the children who are to come. I have no personal animosity against Lardner-Burke but I feel sorry for his children and yours too.'

There were angry faces everywhere. The two security policemen who served the order on me left, leaving an African and a white policeman to take me to Sinoia Prison. They told me to take enough clothes and everything I would need. Gertrude, the police and I went into the bedroom and put those of my belongings which I needed into my suitcase, and took it to the police Land Rover which was in the car park. There were comments from my friends. Some offered to come with me, some said they were determined to work much harder than before and others said that Cold Comfort Farm Society would continue as long as there were members. I felt that the longer I stayed at Cold Comfort Farm, the more disappointed people would be, so I quickly got into the Land Rover and was driven off to Salisbury Central Police Station.

I was taken to a room where there were five African security policemen. They were receiving telephone calls, some asking them to take food to certain places and others requiring them to go out immediately. One of the security policemen was a man who had previously pretended not to know Guy Clutton-Brock and myself. We had taken three friends to see the British High

Commissioner at Salisbury and had noticed this man standing at a corner and making notes. Guy and I decided to approach him. He did not see us going up to him. He was very surprised and startled when Guy asked him, 'What are you doing here?'. He answered in kitchen Kaffir that he was doing nothing, and pretended not to know us. This time he knew me by name, and asked if I still rented a house at Highfield. I reminded him of the occasion when he said he did not know Guy and myself and he said 'What could I have done? The law does not allow me to harass a white man.'

After a little while a number of African security men came into the room pretending to be on other business. They were identifying me. One of them asked how much I earned at Cold Comfort Farm Society. I told him five shillings a week. That annoyed him, because he thougt I was not telling him the truth.

'How can you have so good clothes if you earn that amount?' he asked.

Intending to enlighten him, I told him that most of the clothes I had were given to me by friends. I could have gone on discussing this with him in a friendly way, but his tone made me decide to stop. He had asked me, 'Why don't those friends give some to me?'. My answer, which stopped the discussion, was, 'Because you are busy selling yourself, your country and your people to the white men'. He went out of the room muttering that I was a stubborn man.

The white policeman who had brought me from Cold Comfort Farm Society came in and asked if I could go to the next room to have my finger prints taken. This was done by an African security man. He noticed that my right forefinger is broken and asked what had happened to it. I told him that it was chopped off by a hammermill while we were making silage at Cold Comfort Farm Society.

'Not freedom fighting?' he asked.

'You are right', I said, 'What is going on at Cold Comfort Farm is a peaceful form of freedom fighting, more effective too.'

The white security policeman came to see how we were getting on and said that I should go to Mr Moore's office when we were through. I was shown into the office which was in the same corridor, and sat in a chair in front of the desk. Mr Moore said politely that he wanted me to make a statement about the publication of an article by Chief Tangwena in *The Struggle*, a paper published by the African National People's Union in Rhodesia. He told me that the issue had been banned and it was intended to bring the publishers to court. The statement which I made then and there, said, among other things, that I translated from Shona to English a tape recording of an interview between Chief Tangwena and a reporter of *The Struggle*. I typed the translation and gave it to the reporter. Later, I helped to duplicate the issues of *The Struggle* and to put them together. He asked why I had done that. I replied that I wanted the interview to be widely read and known to many people. The interview, was as follows:-

STRUGGLE: What is the situation at the present time? What are your feelings, and the feelings of your people?

CHIEF TANGWENA: We are angry about what is happening. This land is ours and now they say that it does not belong to Africans. They erected beacons and arrested my people. They beat a pregnant woman. She is still in hospital up to this day. They arrested my people and gave them prison sentences. The people agreed to go to prison. They were ordered to approach the District Commissioner for instructions, but they do not want to discuss the matter with him. When the District Commissioner realised this he decided to round up all the cattle on our land in order to force us to go to Bende. We do not want to go to Bende. The Government will have to build a jail large enough to take all my people. We do not want to go to Bende. We want our cattle back on this land. This may cause trouble but we do not want to fight. We do not want to unjustly accuse anybody. We do not want to shout at anybody. We do not want to throw stones at anybody. We want to live peacefully with everybody. It is the Europeans who have come to disturb us, to destroy our property, to deprive us of the wealth of our land. This is unforgivable. My people are heartsick. These cattle that they are driving away, taking away. They are trying to provoke my people so that they may shoot us with their guns because we are defenceless. Does this help?

STRUGGLE: Why do you not agree to move? How much of your resistance is a matter of principle?

CHIEF TANGWENA: When a person buys a coat, he does not proceed to give it away. This is our land, our home, our heritage. The government is ordering us to forsake our heritage. We will not take bribes. They can keep their money. We will keep what belongs to us. This is an area which we inherited. We do not like Bende. This is our home. Here lie the bodies of our fathers and their fathers

7

before them. Before the African continent was invaded by the Europeans we were here.

STRUGGLE: What is going to happen to the education of the children of the Tangwena people?

CHIEF TANGWENA: If they close the school, I, the children's father, am not educated. If the school which exists for the Tangwena people is destroyed, then the children will have to remain uneducated. We are not educated, nor were our forefathers. Schooling would not have helped us. Of the children of this country who have been to school, many are still suffering. They steal because of lack of jobs. Why should they be educated?

STRUGGLE: Last year when you spoke at the University, you warned the African students of the danger of losing touch with the people and their cause. How do you see this danger?

CHIEF TANGWENA: On that point, the educated young behave like wild animals. We are kicked with the jackboots of the young. Many of them who have passed standard six become policemen. They beat us, they join the CID. Do you think that they are people concerned with building up the country? These children of ours. Are they better than those who are not educated?

STRUGGLE: Do you have any feelings about the political role of the District Commissioner and his relationship with the rural Africans?

CHIEF TANGWENA: The District Commissioner is not a good administrator. I say he is a wolf. He is a killer who wants to swallow the whole country like a snake that swallows a stone it can not chew. The District Commissioner does not want to see an African. He wishes to destroy the African here on earth if this were permitted by God. He hates the African and favours people of his own colour. He is a racist.

STRUGGLE: Do you see yourself, Chief, as a politician and do you see yourself playing a more prominent role in the country?

CHIEF TANGWENA: I am not a politician. I simply want my rights. I think that this country should be freed so that every individual should have a say in his government. If the Europeans were less cruel, and less oppressive in their government, we could determine our lives in consultation with one another. This would be good. The European should not ill treat us, kick us, say 'This belongs to me, that belongs to me, everything belongs to me'. Where was the African living when the Europeans first came? They found us here. Should we live in trees today? Every place that they find to be good they say it belongs to them. Good and fertile land they want for themselves. We Africans have been driven into the mountains. What is there for us to eat? Is this not destructive? It is.

STRUGGLE: It is often said that the African in Rhodesia is ruled by fear. Do you think that this is the case?

CHIEF TANGWENA: We fear because they threaten to shoot us with guns. Where can we go? They arrest us and toast us on fires. They hit us with the butts of their guns. How can you say anything? If you open your mouth you are hit with the butt of a gun. They show you the gun and threaten to shoot. Where can you go? You have no option but to fear the gun that you can see.

STRUGGLE: The World Council of Churches has recently decided to aid liberation movements in Southern

Africa. In a sense this implies endorsement of violent change in societies in which injustice is the rule of the day. What are your feelings about this decision?

CHIEF TANGWENA: There are good people who wish only to help others. We say that they are men of God concerned with saving the souls of others. They are good men who act with courage like that.

STRUGGLE: Given the injustice of the Rhodesian situation, do you see at the moment any alternative to violent change as a means of redress?

CHIEF TANGWENA: Fighting ends suffering. Our oppressors have become subject to other forces. We should say that God will come to us if we seek his grace.

STRUGGLE: Do you see the resettlement of thousands of Africans as being a vital factor in the development of African nationalism in this country?

CHIEF TANGWENA: This question merits serious discussion. If we ignore it, we shall find that we shall become no more than oxen to pull wagons with ropes tied round our necks. These Boers will lead us by the halter. This is the truth. We are troubled. Your God does not seem to like us. We shall always feel that he is unfair. This skin which he gave us makes it difficult for us in this society. Had he given us a white skin, we should have the guns and maybe this country would be better than it is. There would be no provocation.

STRUGGLE: What advice would you give to your fellow Africans in his struggle for this country?

CHIEF TANGWENA: My word of advice to the African people is that we should refrain from fighting unnecessarily. We should have tolerance in this

10

country. Basically, I am not a violent man and I will not commit myself to violence. What we want is a just peace. What we want is social justice. The people must tell the government to stop their cruelty. We want a better system. We want a situation of love.

After signing the statement, I was taken to the office of the man who had brought me from Cold Comfort Farm. He told me that he would take me to Sinoia Prison that afternoon but would like to take photographs of me before we went there. He wrote a requisition for sixteen photographs of me and handed it to the African policeman who took me to a room where the photographs were taken. They asked whether I needed lunch and I gave them some money to buy food for me. After lunch, I was escorted to the toilet and brought back to the room where I had been sitting before. I was asked to go back into the office of the man who brought me from Cold Comfort Farm. He took details of my marital status, size of family and property. At 2.30 p.m., I was asked to fetch my suitcase and put it in the car to travel to Sinoia Prison. I slept most of the way. It took an hour to get there.

At Sinoia, we first went to the offices of the security officer in charge of the Lomagundi area. He then accompanied us to Sinoia Prison, about 200 yards away from his office. There they left me in the gatehouse with the African security man and went to speak to the superintendent of Sinoia Prison. They came back and bade me farewell. Whilst we were standing at the gatehouse the African warders of the prison did not know which one of us was the prisoner. They told me later that they decided to be quiet until one of us left.

11

When this happened, the warders asked me very rudely how much money I had. They demanded that I should hand it to them. They also demanded my wrist-watch, driver's licence and clothes. After stripping myself naked, they threw a prison shirt and pair of shorts at me, bundled my clothes and shoved them into a corner. I protested at that way of handling my clothes and they reminded me that it was not a ZAPU office.

Before I could put on the clothes that had been thrown at me, a more authoritative warder, whom I later learned was referred to as a 'Corporal Warder', arrived and commanded me to come with him. I followed him into the prison yard. He pointed at a prison door and said, 'Go there!' I walked two steps toward the cell, and he made another command, 'Take these blankets! Take that bucket!' With the bundle of clothes, bucket, three blankets and a mat, I was marched naked to cell number 10. There the door was slammed behind me. This frightened me. The door was opened almost immediately, and I was commanded to take the bucket, blankets and clothes to cell number 6. There was an enormous ring fixed to the floor. I thought they would chain me to it.

Then there was a voice as if from heaven, which said, 'Take him to cell number 15'.

They marched me to cell number 15, still naked. Under my armpit I had the three blankets, mat, and the clothes that had been thrown to me. I failed to pick up the bucket quickly and another prisoner was told to carry it for me. In cell number 15 the prison clothes that I had were taken away, and the door was slammed. Five minutes later the door opened and food was thrown in. I had no desire for food and needed rest. I put the food in one corner of the cell and considered how best to use the three blankets and mat that were given to me. The weather was warm so I decided to fold one blanket and use it as a pillow, spread the other over the mat and wrapped myself into the third. I fell asleep immediately and did not wake up until eight o'clock the following morning when the door of the cell was opened.

2
The Reason Why

This imprisonment did not arise out of nothing; it
arose out of who I was and what I had done which was
regarded by the illegal Government of Rhodesia as 'acts
in Rhodesia which would endanger public safety or
disturb or interfere with the maintenance of public
order'.

I was born in Rhodesia on 27 July 1935 at a place
called Madzangwe (where Leopards play) which is on
land owned by St Faith's Mission where my father
was a village headman. St Faith's Mission came into
existence in 1888 to convert the people of the Makoni
tribe to Christianity. It is a Church of England Mission
which was run by an African Catechist from South
Africa, and after the Mashona-land rebellion of 1896
a European missionary came to take charge of the
Mission in 1902. By 1919 a beautiful church had been
constructed by our people and I was baptized in that
church as a baby in August 1935 and later confirmed
as a member of the Church of England in 1949.

My father became headman of the village in 1938.
He was born on the same land in 1880 before the
Mission had started. His father and his father's father
were all born at the same place. We are descendants
of the Makoni tribe which is believed to have moved
from a place known as Chiriri, supposed to be in

Tanzania. Our tribe moved southwards from Tangan-
yika in the twelfth century in search of a place to bury
their King. The tribe found such a place at Chinyudze
after crossing the Zambezi River and walking four
hundred miles southwards. This place is on the northern bank of the Rusape River.

The Wa Nhewa Tribe, of which the Tangwena people
are a part, had settled in this area before my ancestors.
There were many elephants in the area which provided
food for our people. When one such elephant was
killed and shared between the Wa Nhewa and our tribe
a marital relationship was agreed to. In our customs,
then as now, the soft meat of the back of an animal
is given to one's mother-in-law. The Wa Nhewa chose
this portion of the beast and thus became the provid-
ers of the brides to our tribe.

My mother is a descendant of the Wa Nhewa tribe.
So I am a native of this area from both maternal and
paternal descent. By the time of my birth, the area,
as well as the country, had been occupied by the
British people and our land then belonged to St Faith's
Mission. Before this, my tribe had shown the ancestors
of the Tangwena tribe how to make fire by friction
from rubbing two pieces of wood together. From this
they were called by the ancestors of the Tangwena
people 'the Makoni' meaning 'clever men' from the
Shona word 'Mukoni'.

Our tribe took part in the 1896 revolt against the
British and almost defeated them. After the revolt my
father worked for the Rev. Edgar Lloyd as a cook and
accompanied him on long treks to convert people in
the Makoni district and beyond. He told us stories
about his journeys and how Father Lloyd lived on the
same food, *Sadza*, as the people he converted. Those

of the people who became Christians retained the
faith but it was difficult not to worship ancestral
spirits. Father taught us that there was no difference
between God and Mwari. He was the same Being, who,
when worshipped according to Christian rites, is called
God, and according to African rites is called Mwari. In
Christianity his son Christ is our mediator, and in our
rites our ancestors, those who have departed before us,
are our mediators. So the pattern of worship is the
same and the Being worshipped is one.

My father also worked as a cook for Mr G. H. Williams,
a British trader who had set up a prosperous business
in Salisbury. So he served both the early Christians and
traders. He married my mother Erica in 1914. We have
never been able to estimate her age accurately but she
says that she was born when the Makoni people fought
the White Men in 1896. Her father was a herbalist, a
practice which my mother carries on.

I am the last born in a family of six children: three
boys and three girls. My elder brothers are Cyprian
and John. They were born in 1916 and 1918 respectively. They received education up to Standard III for
five years, and went to work in Johannesburg at the
age of fourteen. They went on foot avoiding police
and lions. They discovered that this was a waste of
time and returned home. John became manager of
St Faith's Mission Farm in 1949 when Guy and Molly
Clutton-Brock went to work there and Cyprian was
the farm builder. My sisters' names are Anne, Enid
and Edna. Anne and Edna are married and live at
St Faith's Mission. Enid is not married; she is a house-
maid to a white school-master at Springvale School, a
white children's school near Marandellas in Rhodesia.

As the youngest child in the family I grew up very

much protected and tended to be spoilt. I did not know my brothers until they came home from Johannesburg on holiday in 1942. Through their absence I lost the opportunity to learn from them many of the things that young brothers learn from their elder brothers. I felt the disadvantage of too much protection when I went to school in 1942. We had to walk three miles from Madzangwe to St Faith's Mission School. There were no older brothers or sisters to take my hand. They had finished school. My youngest sister, Edna, was still too young to help. So, with other children we had to walk six miles a day five days a week, to and from school. We left home to go to school at 5 a.m. and returned at 3 p.m. We rarely had any meals during the day. Sometimes we only had supper.

We were required to work in the Mission garden to help the gardener grow vegetables. We never ate these vegetables. Sometimes we stole them and were punished. We were told that it was a sin to steal, but we stole to keep our body and soul together. At school we learnt to read and write, and to do arithmetic. We learnt scripture and to use our minds. We were taught to be better than everybody—to compete. This we did, because it is what our superiors wanted us to do. It was also what our parents expected us to do, but it did not agree with the teaching of God. The scriptures teach us to share, to give one of two coats to those who have none. We were too young to think about this, so we did as we were told. I was amazed by the difference between what we believe and how we put it into practice. As human beings, Church leaders were no exception.

Apart from education and the Religious work, St Faith's did some medical work, to help the 300 families who lived on the Mission, but before 1949 it did not concern itself with the welfare of the villagers nor make provision for their material well-being. Every family was allotted 8 acres of land on which to grow crops to feed the family and to provide cash to buy clothes, pay the children's school fees, support the work of the Church, pay personal tax and meet the many demands of life. The soil was poor and the people lacked modern agricultural know-how to make the best use of the land allotted to them.

Before the period when 8 acres of land was allocated to each family, our people practised shifting agriculture. They could go from one piece of land to another and were able to grow enough crops to feed themselves. They did not have to find the money to pay school fees or support church workers. These were not necessary. The land at first gave enough return but under continuous use the returns from the land diminished. Male members of families soon decided to go to towns to find cash with which to pay tax. Some fathers left their families at home for long periods and returned to them for very short periods on leave. Others went for a long time and set up second families in towns. This raised moral problems which the Church could not solve.

As head of the village, my father was concerned with some of these problems. Members of the village went to him for advice—he helped as best as he could. He was required to collect personal tax from all adult men in the village and take it to the nearest government tax collector. He kept it under the roof of the house before he took it to Rusape, a distance of nine miles on foot. If he was late he could either be kept waiting until the next convenient time or be sent away. He was often told that he had not collected enough money, should take back what he had, and come back when he had collected the amount that the official decided on. He was neither thanked nor paid for his services. He was required to take off his hat in the presence of the official; to sit down on the floor when the official was speaking to him; not to answer back, and to refer to him as N'Kosi—Chief. He was humiliated in return for the services that he rendered. He was a slave to the system.

When my father could not take the personal tax the assistant headman did so. Once he had to collect more tax on the way. He was offered and drank some beer. On arriving at the Native Commissioner's office at Rusape, the Native Commissioner was displeased by the smell of beer in his breath. He ordered him to stand under the running water from a gutter. What could be done to seek redress? The Native Commissioner was there to protect the natives. His office dealt with all the natives' matters but did not understand the natives. Was this benign ignorance?

My father sought refuge in his inability to talk to the White Man in English, as if the white man he was dealing with did not understand my father's language. When pressed further to seek redress my father said 'It is a waste of time, the accused will be the judge. You know what the judgement will be.' I knew this feeling hurt my father as much as it hurt me. I was only eleven years old when this happened in 1946. Feelings affect both the young and the old.

Three years later, Guy and Molly Clutton-Brock and their daughter Sally came to live and work at St Faith's Mission. During their stay there one of the St Faith's school teachers went to Rusape. On his way back he was arrested by a white landowner for trespassing. Guy and Molly helped to get him out of prison and to have his case properly heard in Court. This encouraged us, but brought rebuke to Guy and Molly from the Rusape white landowners. A man had at last arrived whose life and that of his friends had a profound effect on my own. Through Guy and Molly the gospels became to bear some meaning. It was and is not very easy to follow the path that he and Molly trod.

In 1950 I finished Primary school at St Faith's Mission and was selected with three other boys to attend Goromonzi School. It was the only school in the country that offered education to Africans up to Cambridge School Certificate. By 1956 the school offered Higher School Certificate education leading on to University work. I attended Goromonzi school from 1951 to 1957. During this period we formed the Makoni Students Association which had a lot of influence on the people of Makoni district. It invited African leaders to address meetings and to seek redress to some of the bad laws which existed in our district.

On leaving school in 1957 I went to work at St Faith's Mission where a successful co-operative farming scheme had been developed. In 1960 when the church closed the co-operative I joined the Civil Service of the Federation of Rhodesia and Nyasaland and worked as an Administrative and Executive Officer in the training branch of the Department of Conservation and Expansion in the Ministry of Agriculture. There were problems there which had to be put right. When I joined I was offered, and accepted, a wage of £15 a month. European boys of inferior education to myself were receiving £45 per month. On drawing this fact to the Authority's attention my wage was raised to £27.10 a month. This problem did not affect me alone.

In 1961 we formed the Southern Region Association and I became its secretary up to 1965. Through it we battled for our salaries and conditions of service. Our case was straightforward and we put it clearly to the Federal Public Services Commission. African State Registered Nurses working at Harare Hospital received a wage of £27 a month, when European nurses of the same qualifications were receiving £56 a month. The difference in wages was due to the colour of the nurses' skin. By the time that I left the Service in 1965 nurses were starting on a salary of £60 a month. My wages were £85 a month. This was in return for drinking tea and doing two hour's work a day. This bored me and was meaningless. So I left the Service.

During the negotiations to end the Federation of Rhodesia and Nyasaland in 1963 three of us were sent to a session of the Victoria Falls Conference which ended the Federation. There I first met Dr Kaunda and Mr John Mwanakatwe, and talked to them about the Service. We found them most reasonable and were most impressed with Dr Kaunda's humanity and humility. On leaving the Conference, two European colleagues said that the Dr Kaunda that we had met was not the one that was written about in the newspapers. We came to England twice to negotiate the terms of the break-up of the Federal Civil Service. It was during one of these visits, in December 1963, that we discussed the idea of starting the Cold Comfort Farm Society.

I would have left the Civil Service at the end of the Federation, but it was not good to do so before everybody else had decided what to do. The Rhodesian Government employment offers were not attractive for many Africans and particularly those who had been in the Federal Civil Service who had worked very hard to improve their conditions of service.

I could only bear my new job for two years, consisting as it did of two hours work a day and a lot of tea. At the end of 1965 we had to get started on the Cold Comfort Farm Society. It was a new experience to work with unemployed youth in a community development venture of which I was Chairman, up to the time of my detention.

At about the same time as the Cold Comfort Farm Society started I became director of the Nyafaru Development Company. I had been asked to do so in order to help with difficulties which the Company was facing. It was during this period when I was managing the company's school that I met Chief Rekayi Tangwena. The school was educating his people's children. We wanted to start higher classes and to find staff to teach in these classes. As school manager it was my responsibility to be a go-between for the parents and the Government; to appoint the teachers; chair parent/ teachers meetings and to see that the school ran well.

During this time the Tangwena crisis started and Chief Rekayi Tangwena asked me to help him. My concern had always been the development of people, helping them to make proper use of the land and to live constructively and in harmony as human beings. I accepted that politics cannot be divorced from real life. How can it when the very existence of men depends upon political decisions? I do not think that I could be referred to as a militant politician. I was a member of the African National Congress and attended its inaugural meeting as a delegate representing the Makoni Students Association in 1957. I supported

ZAPU but could not be a member of it because Civil servants could not be members of any political party. When ZANU was formed, some of my friends became members of it. I was horrified by this split but found it difficult to support one lot of my friends and not the other, so I kept the dangerous middle-of-the-road course and supported those of my friends who came to me in their difficulties, regardless of which of the two parties they belonged to. Am I a communist? I agree with my lawyer that I 'could never be regarded as in any sense communist or communistically inclined except by those sort of persons who would regard as such anyone trying to put the Christian Gospel into practice.' I hardly knew what communism was until I came to Britain in November 1972.

A family of my own? Yes. I met Flora Musengezi in August 1957 at a dance in the community centre at St Faith's Mission. She was the daughter of the African priest who had just come from Bonda Mission, another Church of England Mission, forty miles east of St Faith's. She was in the final year of her training to become a nurse and I was just about to leave Goromonzi school. As with most African girls at home I had to wait a year before she agreed to be my wife. We got married on 21 November 1959 without her parents' permission. Her father found it difficult to let us marry in the midst of a controversy between the Church and the Farm which was going on at St Faith's at that time. My brother John, the farm manager, and the Rev. Arthur Lewis, the priest in charge, were at the centre of the controversy. Being the farm manager's brother, the Rev. A.R. Lewis thought I did not support the Church and therefore could not marry the priest's daughter. He tried to stop our marriage on the grounds that I did not go to church regularly. He brought up the acting Bishop to St Faith's to try to stop the marriage. Flora's father never mentioned to, me, herself, or other people in the village, that he did not want me to marry his daughter. Flora's mother and my mother were good friends and went to the Mother's Union together—so I could not understand what the Rev. A.R. Lewis was trying to do. I got hold of the Canons of the Diocese of Mashonaland and learnt that no priest could stop the marriage of adults. The then Bishop of Mashonaland, the late Cecil Alderson, was back from leave, so we went to see him in terms of the Canons, and got his permission to marry, to the disappointment of the Rev. Arthur Lewis. This was my first experience of beating an opponent at his own game. On meeting the Rev. A.R. Lewis at Umtali after Flora's death, he said he was sorry.

Our son Edwin was born on June 1960, Euphemia, our daughter, came in February 1962 and Martin, our son, in June, 1964. We had moved from Highfields, an African township in Salisbury, to live at Cold Comfort Farm when Flora died on 11 December 1966. I was shocked by her death on a Sunday morning. Guy and I were on our way to see the Tangwena people; before we got there we were called back home and told to go to Harare Hospital. Flora had passed away when we arrived there. I was never able to say goodbye. Perhaps it was meant to be like that because I felt her presence and even thought I saw her long after she had died. Occasionally she comes back and my present wife, Gertrude, often answers when I call her Flora.

Gertrude Munonyara and I were married at Salisbury prison. We met in July 1968 through Mrs Stella Madzimbamuto. Gertrude was training to be a State nurse at Harare and Stella was in charge of a ward there. It took a year before Gertrude decided to marry me—being ten years younger than me and becoming a farmer's wife was not really encouraging. She has not yet told me what was attractive. Perhaps it was love, because when Rudo, our daughter, was born in 1970, Gertrude gave her the name which means 'love' in Shona. It was certainly neither security nor want of a better life which made Gertrude marry me because she knew she would get none of these.

In 1969, when we fell in love and decided to marry, the Tangwena crisis was at its height. She knew I could be arrested and sent to prison at any time. The detention laws had been passed and many people were detained in prison, and she realised it could happen to me at any time. I don't think it was a surprise to her when in November 1970 I followed the path that many African leaders had trod.

3

My Concern for People

My concern for people can best be seen in my involve-
ment in the problems that faced various groups of our
people. It started when I was eleven years old from
seeing the difficulties that my father faced as a headman and the problems that this brought to the family.
There were many headmen like my father, so my mind
was turned to them as well. It made me think in a wider
context: it was not only our family where the father
was headman, but the problem affected many families.
As a headman my father was under Chief Makoni,
whose traditional authority had gradually disappeared
and had been invested in the Native Commissioner, at
present known as the District Commissioner. It was
obvious to me that the wish of the people could no
longer be expressed through the Chiefs, who had then
become puppets of the sophisticated bureaucracy. It
was necessary to do something about this, and the
Makoni Students' Association played its part.

The Makoni Students' Association started at
Goromonzi in 1953. Alfred Mwamuka, a man who had
taught me at St Faith's Mission in 1950, was then
teaching me again at Goromonzi. His father had been
a prosperous member of the District, and Alfred himself had had a university education at Fort Hare in
South Africa. He had had numerous difficulties at the

Native Commissioner's Office at Rusape which did not like educated Africans. His example in dealing with these difficulties inspired those of us who had been following his path. Stephen Matewa and I asked him to help us to draft the constitution of the Makoni Students' Association. Stephen Matewa was my classmate from 1948 to 1954. We were at school together at St Faith's Mission and then at Goromonzi School. When he left Goromonzi he went to learn to teach at St Augustine's Mission. He later taught at St Faith's Mission and became headmaster of that school in 1962. When he left his post at St Faith's Mission in 1966, he became headmaster and managing director of the Nyafaru Development Company. He is now headmaster of the Epiphany Mission.

The Makoni Students' Association concerned itself with studying the problems that affected the people of the Makoni District. These problems were caused by government legislation—the African Affairs Act and the Land Husabndry Act. We considered the Pass Laws and intended to seek practical solutions to these problems. It was in terms of the African Affairs Act that my father was headman. He was not paid anything for being headman. After the interview between the Makoni Students' Association and the late Mr Norman Straw M.P., African headmen began to be paid a small amount for wages.

During the same time the Land Husbandry Act was in operation. This required many African families who lived in African Reserves, (now called the Tribal Trust Lands) to use poor land made available to them. They had to make contour-ridges on arable land, reduce the number of stock that they owned and not to cultivate mixed crops. Ill-trained agricultural demonstrators were employed to supervise this system. It had never been discussed with the people and could be implemented in a better way to achieve a different purpose. Those people who did not construct contour-ridges on their lands, or who mixed their crops were punished by the Land Development Officer and the Native Commissioner. If the crops were mixed, for instance if a maize crop was mixed with rapoko, the agricultural demonstrator would arbitrarily demand that one of the crops be pulled out. If both crops were good, this was obviously a loss to the farmer, who had put a lot of money and labour to grow them. There was nothing in agriculture to show that the practice of mixing crops was wrong. This was enough to prove the inefficiency and bad advice of the Land Development Officers, given through ill-trained agricultural demonstrators. The Makoni Student Association argued that the Land Development Officer was not efficient, if he waited until the crops had grown big before deciding to have them pulled out. He should have been there at the time of planting, to advise the farmer how to plant the crops and thus avoid the mistake, if it was a mistake, that he had to correct later.

The problem of destocking was also interesting. Many people kept their wealth in the form of livestock. On an average, families had up to 20 head of cattle; these had plenty of grass to graze before the establishment of the Native Reserves. Cattle were very fat, and used for milk, for meat and to plough. When the families were moved into the Reserves, these areas became over-crowded. The land available for grazing could no longer sustain the large number of cattle. The problem of over-grazing cropped up: the number of cattle had to be reduced. The procedure was that the Land Development Officer would order all the cattle to be brought to a central area where they were dipped. Each family possessed a card, showing the number of cattle it was allowed to own; if there were too many, the Land Development Officer would brand the number in excess, sometimes the best. These cattle had to be sold by auction to European farmers or other entrepreneurs. Low prices were paid for them. It did not require Mao Tse Tung to point out the iniquity of this policy.

The Makoni Students' Association pointed this out, to the fascination of the students who came to the conferences. Those students went home and told their parents, and the following conferences were attended by many parents as well as students. We then had to widen the definition of 'student' to include all those who were learning to live through the difficulties of the Rhodesian situation in the mid-1950s.

The Youth League, a forerunner to the African National Congress, became interested in the activities of the Makoni Students' Association. We invited its chairman, Mr Robert Chikerema, to the Makoni Students' Association conference, which was held at Chingono in May 1957. We also invited the local MP, Mr Norman Straw, to the same conference. As well as being a member of parliament, Mr Straw was a local European landowner. We went to his farm to talk to him about the headmen and it was then that we invited him to talk to the conference. I offered to meet him at the Makoni village church and to show him the way to Chingono village. He was travelling in a Rover 90 car. It was easy for him to go from his farm to Makoni village, because the road was good. From there on he began to curse me for not advising the people in the Reserve to make better roads. I pointed out that it was his duty, as a Member of Parliament, to do so.

We were interested to let him see the extent of the problems that the rural people had to face. At the conference Mr Robert Chikerema talked critically about the Land Husbandry Act, and blamed it on the ignorance of the Government. Mr Norman Straw talked about the same thing, and blamed failure of the Land Husbandry Act on the African people. The Conference asked how the Africans could be blamed for a law that they had never been consulted about and which was made in their absence. They also asked how Mr Straw could claim to represent the African people of Makoni District in Parliament if he did not know the problems of the people or know the way to Chingono village, which was a part of his constituency and only 30 miles away from his home.

Conferences of the Makoni Students' Association were held three times a year at different parts of the District. The number of 'old' students increased. The African National Congress, which was formed in July 1957, began to fulfil the role of the Makoni Students' Association by holding meetings more often at the request of the people of the District. Representations were made, by members of the African National Congress, to the authorities, to change the system and the Land Husbandry Act. These representations were ignored and conflict started. People in the District could no longer see the need for agricultural demonstrators, whom they regarded as tools through which the Government imposed retrogressive Acts. The demonstrators' houses were burnt down, and, in some areas it became very difficult for them to work. This difficulty continued during my employment in the Department of Conservation and Extension in the early sixties.

During this time it was very interesting to read some of the official reports of what went on at the Weya Reserve, a part of Makoni District, and I thanked goodness that I was not involved in solving these problems created by the Rhodesian Government.

In 1956 and '57 my life was divided equally between my school work at Goromonzi School, and trying to solve the problems of our people, as shown by the Makoni Students' Association and the African National Congress. By this time I had become Chairman of the Makoni Students' Association. The eyes of the detectives were no doubt set upon me; no doubt their reports were being checked with the Principal of the school, a man who learnt to dislike me intensely. He made me a prefect against his will and told us that prefects were the eyes of the Principal. I knew what he meant but interpreted it to mean also that the prefects were the eyes of the pupils.

In June 1956 the school football and netball teams went to play against secondary schools in the Eastern Districts at Umtali. We went by train on Friday night and played during the weekend; we returned to school on the night train on Sunday. We felt very tired on Monday morning because we had had very little sleep on the train and some of us decided to sleep instead of going to school. The Principal went round the dormitories taking down the names of those who did not attend school that day and punished them. My punishment was to write an essay of not less than 300 words on Good Citizenship. I wrote as frankly as I could, pointing out that there were two classes of citizens in our country: the upper class which consisted of Europeans was protected by the law, and the lower class which consisted of Africans was victimized by the law. The lower class had to scramble for the worst that was provided for them while the upper class lived an extraordinarily good life provided for them by the lower class. The lower class was subjected to inhuman laws, had to travel in over-crowded public transport on the railways, and received poor education, making them only suitable for employment as second-class citizens. I pointed out that I knew what Good Citizenship meant, and that probably my understanding of it and my desire for what it should be, were different from that of the Principal. Being European, the Principal could never appreciate how I, as an African, felt about such citizenship.

Two days after I had submitted this essay to the Principal, I was summoned to his office and rebuked for writing it as I did. I told the Principal that what I wrote was the truth and reality of our citizenship as I saw it. I told him that I knew he would disagree because he was one of those who were benefiting from the system. After a severe telling-off, the Principal told me that he would never do anything to help me.

The next time that the Principal called the prefects to a meeting to brief them on their responsibilities, I expected the school captain would let him know that there were worms in our maize meal. Towards the end of the meeting when this was not done—I thought it was my responsibility, as one of the eyes of the pupils, to do so. The Principal furious, thinking it was not true, demanded that I should prove it. At lunch the following day I asked the school pupils to collect the worms so that I could take them to the Principal.

The presentations was unceremonious and the Principal, thinking that I was a trouble-maker, rebuked me. I tried in vain to explain to him that if I was a trouble-maker I would have put the worms into the maize meal in the first instance, but as this was not so I could not agree with him. Later, however, the meal was returned, and continued use of worm-free meal brought happiness to the school. I was not trying to cause trouble but prevented it.

Real trouble came when the students said they did not like their examination results to be called out publicly, then the Principal did not hesitate to point his fingers at me. I happened to have been one of the prefects on duty that week, and the rule for evening meals was that the dining-room door had to be closed ten minutes after the bell rang. Those who were late would be shut out. They would be unable to answer their names at the roll-call which took place during the meals. I was reluctant to close the door if anyone was running towards it because I did not want people to be punished. However, the school-master on duty closed the door and ordered me to write down the names of those who were late. Unknowingly I wrote the names on a piece of paper the other side of which carried an announcement to students to boo at the Principal if he announced the results publicly. I realised my mistake after I had handed the paper to the school-master. I could not do anything other than bear the responsibility of the mistake. The Principal was forewarned, but insisted on calling out the results publicly. He was booed at by the whole school. He retaliated by punishing all the school except the prefects. I identified myself with the rest of the school and was punished together with the rest of the pupils.

The Principal asked me why, and I told him that it was because he had punished me before. He hit me with a stick during the punishment and that endeared me to the rest of the school. When the punishment was over, and the Principal had realised that his efforts had failed, he ordered the rest of the school to disperse, and, as the school was closing that day, he asked me (who was required to answer questions before the local police) to stay behind.

There were two African teachers at that time teaching at Goromonzi; one of them came to me and advised me to keep my head; the other intimidated me. One of these men is now an inspector of African schools. The Principal interviewed me before the police arrived and discovered that he would make a fool of himself if I had to talk with the police. So the interview did not take place in his presence. Afterwards I demanded that the police should take me to Salisbury to meet my brother John, who was at the Agricultural Show. This to my surprise was done. Under the usual practice I would have been left stranded at school.

I am describing this, which could be regarded as the normal relationship between pupils and Principals at any school, because it appeared later to be one of the reasons why I was detained. The essay that I wrote for the Principal was read to me when I appeared before the Secret Review Tribunal which reviewed my case of detention three times, and this essay was given as evidence of my supposed hatred of the white men in Rhodesia.

The co-operative work at St Faith's Mission started in 1949. Before this time, young men had drifted to the towns to seek work. There were more women there than men. Privisions of the Land Husbandry Act applied here as in the rest of the country. The women of the village were required to cultivate the land and look after their families and livestock. As the Mission land was regarded as a European farm, the Land Inspectors were more courteous and the people were cushioned by the Priest-in-charge, who often was away from the place, because his work required him to visit and supervise many sub-Stations which were run by the Central Mission. The Church was under pressure to make productive use of the land agriculturally, in order primarily to meet the needs of feeding the boarding school and provide adequate food for the villagers. A number of men were employed by the Mission to look after the Mission's head of cattle which provided milk for the Sisters and the Priest-in-charge. They could hardly produce much more, and it must have been becoming a questionable proposition to let the situation continue.

A very wise decision was made to ask Guy Clutton-Brock to lead the communal side of the Mission; this changed the whole outlook of the place. It gave us, the young people of the village and those of the District, a new horizon and something to live for. The effect of this work was still felt even at the time that the Pearce Commission, long after Guy Clutton-Brock left the place, came to assess our opinions in Rhodesia. The Pearce Commission reports as follows:

'The African population in the Manica Province is relatively sophisticated and politically well-informed and active. There were few parts of the Province which could be termed backward and this is undoubtedly due to the strong influence of many different Missions in the Province, a number of which had been politically forceful. For example

St Faith's Mission at Rusape was the former base of Mr Guy Clutton-Brock, while the United American Methodist Mission at Old Umtali and the Methodist Mission at Mount Selinda have produced Bishop Muzorewa, leader of the African National Council and the Rev. Ndabaningi Sithole respectively.'

In 1958 when I joined the staff of St Faith's Mission Farm much inspiring progress had been made. Most of the men had drifted back to the village from the towns. The place was economically viable. It was then able to produce all the food necessary to feed the school and families of the village, and to sell most of the surplus through the Co-operative Store, which it had established. A carpentry shop and a butchery, had also been established. Through these, people's clothes and furniture needs were provided at reasonably low prices. The profits made were paid back to all members of the Co-operative. A communal farm had been set up, on which many of the men who had come back from the towns could be employed at wages much higher than those given to farm-labourers in the rest of the country.

A Community Centre was set up for meetings, recreation, social functions, studying and accommodation for visitors, passers-by, and young men and women who came to learn and work at the place. A new tempo of activity could be seen at the place; a sense of belonging and security was established. The village Committee made all the decisions of the place; the Priest-in-charge was Chairman of the Committee and in his absence the assistant Priest took the Chair. All Heads of Departments were members of the Village Committee, including the Head of the school, the Head of the village, the Head of the farm, the Head of the Community of the Resurrection, and the Head of the Mukwapasi Clini. The Village Committee co-ordinated activities of the whole place, which acted as one, under the Priest-in-charge. This was the situation from the beginning of the Co-operative work at St Faith's up to 1959 when the Diocese of Mashonaland took over the running of the Farm, and later decided to close the place for reasons which were not convincingly explained to the people.

During the period of progress racial harmony had been established through the charismaristic leadership of Guy Clutton-Brock. It was normal, then, to refer to people just as people, not as white or black people. The Leader of the Farm was a black man, and the labourers included a white man, the late Cedric Wildman. The Head of the school was sometimes a white man and sometimes a black man. The Head of the Mission was always a white man, but that was decided by people outside the Mission, who worked for the Diocese of Mashonaland, far removed from the people.

The success and failure of the people was not discussed or determined in terms of the colour of their skin, and nor were their wages. So all men became equal in the eyes of everybody. This was against Government policy, which was designed to exalt the white man. No doubt the Government influence was brought to bear in the decision to close the place down. The African National Congress leaders had seen St Faith's become an example of what could be practised in the rest of the country. They came there often to attend weekend courses in agriculture, education, law. They also came to attend discussion groups which considered such matters as African customs, religion and anthropology. The presence of the ANC members there was given by the Church as one of the reasons why the Government was afraid of its continuation.

Guy Clutton-Brock decided to leave after he had been given an assurance by the then Bishop of the Diocese of Mashonaland that St Faith's would be continued. Before the farm work was stopped there were widows and old families who could not provide for themselves, and the Farm took care of these people, gave them food, and repaired their houses. It was the duty of the Community, which provided these through the headman under the tribal system. The Village Committee rightly took over this responsibility, as headmen were members of the Village Committee. It was interesting to see how a tribal system, which was functioning under the strain of an exploitive system, could be rejuvenated and made to function harmoniously under a modern economic system. The Heads of the village and their counsellors, who had groaned under the exploitive system to find money to pay their personal taxes, could then do so quite easily; and they could deliver their taxes to the authorities in a car owned by the Community. It became possible for families which had broken up due to the absence of the father to live together again.

When the new control, which was imposed by the diocese, failed to carry this work through, and forced the closure of the Co-operative work, my faith in the Church leaders was greatly strained. After the sale of the assets, I learned, from reliable sources, that the Church had made a net profit of £11,000. The Church refused to use this money for the benefit of the people of St Faith's to help them to set themselves up on new land that had been allocated to them after the closure of the Co-operative.

The words of the Sermon on the Mountain that had
been so often preached in the Church, had probably
been misinterpreted by those who heard them. Now
they were made clear. Very often we were told that
'Blessed are the poor in spirit, for theirs is the Kingdom of Heaven'. The people of St Faith's had created
some material comfort—this was lawfully taken by
the Church and the people became poor both in spirit
and material well-being. It becomes difficult to argue
in favour of the lives and actions of some Christian
leaders in Africa. Nonetheless, those of us who belived
that the best way to preach the Gospel was to live
according to it, sought a new venture, which led us to
the Cold Comfort Farm Society.

The experience that we had acquired through work
at St Faith's was our only treasure. A seed had been
sown which could grow, and after that growth could
be scattered to produce more seeds. No one could
take away from us what we possessed in our minds—
we were prepared to try again in a situation divorced
from outside control. Five years of work in the Civil
Service served as a breathing space and gave me some
understanding and knowledge of the operation of
government institutions.

The problem facing our people continually knocked
in my mind and could not escape my notice. Though
we had achieved equal pay and conditions for people
holding equal qualifications in the Civil Service, we
could not escape the application of discriminatory
laws. We were still required to carry our registration
and identification papers, to live in areas set aside for
Africans and to use separate facilities. This served as
our common identity with our people, no matter how
educated or rich an African could be. When it came to

discrimination his lot was determined for him by the colour of his skin.

In 1964, when it was generally known that I would be leaving the Government, and had started to find young men in Highfield who would be prepared to set an example in their country's development, the Rhodesian security police arrested me at 3 a.m. at my home at Highfield, and took me to the Central Police Station for questioning. I told them all that they wanted to know about myself and my friends, such as Monica Brewer, Patricia Chater, Sheila Graham, Ralph Ibbot and Guy Clutton-Brock. I was released at noon the same day after my finger prints had been taken. This was at the height of the feud between the African Nationalist Parties, and although the idea of setting up the Cold Comfort Farm Society seemed dangerous to the regime six years later, it did not appear dangerous at this time; for the regime thought that we would be unable to find suitable land near Salisbury, as all land was held by Europeans.

Two years later, we had established ourselves as a Society whose aims were 'to promote understanding, friendship, co-operation and development among the people through undertaking projects designed to increase production from natural resources,' on land which was held my Michael and Eileen Haddon. The Rhodesian uniformed police began to harass us. Under our constitution, we appeared to be employed by Michael and Eileen Haddon, who were also members of the Society. When this was no longer so the police came to see if we were contravening the Land Apportionment Act. They discovered that though we were running the Farm differently from other farmers, we were acting within the terms of the Land Apportionment Act. They told us that we had found a loop-hole in the Act. They were afraid that similar societies would be set up to occupy land which had been set aside for use by Europeans. They blocked this possibility by introducing the Land Tenure Act which made it impossible for any African to make use of land in a 'European area'.

From the very beginning, Cold Comfort Farm Society sought to establish itself on the basis of equality among all races. There was no reference to a person by the colour of his skin, and very often when European and police visitors were referred to the Chairman, they came to my room expecting to find a white man. Some accepted this as the way in which things should be, and others disliked it, because they saw it as a threat to European domination. Our desire was not to dominate the Europeans but to prove to them that, given the right circumstances and good leadership, neglected African boys and girls would be able to organise their social and economic lives for their benefit better than it was organised for them by the minority Government whose interests were to suppress them.

The constitution of the society placed the day to day management of the society between the general meetings in the hands of the Chairman. Theoretically he could dissolve the Society, and was the Society in between meetings. To comply with the terms of the Land Apportionment Act, it was necessary for the Society to have three Trustees; these were Lord Acton, Mr G.C. Grant, and Bishop Kenneth Skelton. We had these to appoint a European to hold a controlling vote at general meetings. This European was Guy Clutton-Brock, who was also Treasurer of the Society.

These four Europeans held liberal views and got on well with Africans. They have since been forced to leave Rhodesia, either through the direct action of the government, or from their own conscience as British citizens, because they did not want to live in an illegally controlled British Colony.

African young men, chosen by members of the Society, became leaders of the various activities of the enterprise which was run by the Society. William Ncube was the vice-Chairman, Moven Mahachi was deputy vice-Chairman. Charles Nyandoro became Leader responsible for the arable lands. Willard Mutiwasekwa and Sidney Kwelekwele shared responsibility for looking after livestock. Aggreson Kazingizi and Robert Mariot were responsible for the machinery. Amon Shonge, and his wife Elizabeth Shonge were responsible for the household. Arthur Chadzingwa, after graduating in economics from the University of Rhodesia in 1969, came to look after the accounts, and would have probably taken over from Guy, as Treasurer of the Society. Under this framework which had been created by the members of the Society for themselves, it was not surprising that the Society operated the Farm smoothly and that individual members of the Society worked with enthusiasm; this was only after they had seen in reality that nobody but themselves was benefiting from the fruits of their labour. Those who ran the various aspects of the enterprise tried to do so to the best of their ability. It was quite noticeable to them that different members contributed more and others less. This was for the benefit of the Society.

The money that was used to buy Cold Comfort Farm had been donated by Christian individuals in different parts of the world. Perhaps none of these individuals could be regarded as very rich in any sense. Members of the Cold Comfort Farm Society accepted this gesture as a challenge to them that they in turn must help those in their community who were less privileged than themselves, and in need of the basics of life—food, clothes, and shelter. We therefore sold our farm produce as cheaply as was possible, providing the basic food needs for those who lived round us in the African townships of Harare, Highfield, Mufakose, Kambuzuma, and Dzivaresekwa. Their demand for vegetables was much greater than our supply, but we never used this as an incentive to make a profit. We charged fair prices that our customers could afford. Therefore most of our produce was bought by the poor, who could bear the discomfort of walking long distances on foot in the early hours of the morning, and sometimes arrived at the land at 3 a.m., made fires under the trees near the garden to warm themselves until we were ready to show them where they could pick the produce. All customers were treated the same; those who were poor enjoyed it because they could pick the best that their money could buy. Those who were rich also enjoyed the experience of picking fresh vegetables for themselves and being one with other people. The poor cried when the Farm was closed down by the illegal regime in 1971.

After the day's work after supper, members of the Society would meet to discuss the next day's work and problems which they had faced during that day. The leaders of the livestock, the arable land, machinery, the household, would allocate duties to those whom they worked with. Afterwards the members could discuss any problem that they wanted. This gave an opportunity for other members of the Society to suggest how to solve the problems. It also gave a Leader an opportunity to see where his attention was most needed.

Following this, members could make individual comments on any other member who was not doing his best. He would be called upon to state his case. This was taken seriously by everybody and there was a genuine desire to help those who needed any kind of help. Very often it was of a moral nature, but sometimes the help was economic, such as assisting a member to help his parents to establish themselves in a new area. It was sometimes of a legal nature, to help other members of the community, perhaps victims of the law, to express themselves through lawyers. At other times the assistance was of a political nature, to help those who had been placed in the wrong by the action of the Government through Parliament, such as the Tangwena people and the Mtema people, and many others. All this meant that the Chairman of the Cold Comfort Farm Society had often to be away from the Farm. It gave the vice- and deputy vice-chairman an opportunity to run the Farm themselves, which proved essential when the Chairman was detained, and they showed that they could successfully carry on.

The struggle of the Tangwena people which is still going on at the moment is a very clear example of lack of concern of the wishes of the ordinary people. In 1965 the Tangwena people traditionally elected Rekeyi Tangwena as successor to their Chieftainship. In obedience to the laws of the country, they made their choice known to the authorities, who then wanted to use this as a lever to move the Tangwena people from their area, or to place them under a labour agreement. The authorities agreed to appoint Rekayi Tangwena as the Chief on either of these two conditions. To the Tangwena people these two conditions were the same; if they agreed to move away they would move as a tribe, and if they accepted the labour agreement, they would ultimately be moved away as individuals and thereby destroy their tribal identity. Neither of the choices was acceptable to the Tangwena people, and they decided to stay on the land whether their Chief was recognised by the government or not.

A lot of pressure was put on Rekayi Tangwena to make him leave the area, on the grounds that if he moved his people could be coerced to follow him. Rekayi Tangwena was brought before the Criminal Court, charged with breaking the Land Apportionment Act. He was sentenced to three months imprisonment, or to pay a fine of £30. His appeal was upheld by the Appeal Court, and his sentence and convictions were quashed.

Afterwards Mr Clifford Dupont, President of the illegal Government of Rhodesia, who was then illegally exercising the powers of the Governor, made a proclamation in terms of the Land Apportionment Act to evict 36 of the Tangwena families, including Rekayi Tangwena. He sent officials and employees of the Ministry of Internal Affairs to carry out the evictions. They arrested the Chief and rusticated him at a place more than 12 miles from his home, and then destroyed the homes of the 36 families mentioned in the proclamation. In the process they destroyed some homes of people who were legally resident in the area. The matter was referred to the Chief's lawyers, and the Government agreed to compensate these families up to $2000. This agreement was made out of court.

When the Land Tenure Act became law in 1970 the Tangwena people were dispossessed of their land, but efforts to evict them have been unsuccessful up to the present time. Three instances appear worth looking at, in connection with the eviction of the Tangwena people.

When it was obvious that the Government would move in to evict the 36 families, all the Tangwena tribe knew that it would be their turn next to be evicted, if the first eviction were successful. They therefore decided not to co-operate with the government officials. They knew the exact date and time that the evictions would take place from employees of government officials. These employees were on the side of the Tangwena people. They themselves were part of the tribe, but could not reveal this to their employers.

The second point is that the Tangwena people knew their area better than the people who were coming to evict them. There is only one small road in the area along which motorists must drive very carefully, particularly during the rainy season. It is impossible to turn round in the road except at three points which are three miles apart. The topography of the area is such that by standing on top of a hill, the Tangwena people can see anybody approaching from any direction. The officials could approach from only one direction and the Tangwena people went into hiding long before those who were hunting them could arrive.

The third point is that during the time that the Chief was rusticated, he decided after three days, to walk to Salisbury to address a meeting of the students at the University of Rhodesia and Epworth Theological College. He did this after holding a press conference in his area, without the Security Police realising it, even though they were patrolling the area. We could see them but they could not see us.

After the address to the students the Chief and I were arrested at Odzi, about 130 miles away from Salisbury, on the way to Umtali, while going to address the students at Old Umtali and St Augustine's Mission. The police officer commanding the Inyanga area travelled from Rusape to Odzi to ask the Chief when he would be returning to his area. When news of the arrest of the Chief was heard at Odzi, a crowd of policemen gathered to see the Chief and to wish him courage in his stand against the government. As the Chief and I drove from the Camp the crowd stood at attention and saluted the Chief. When we were detained at the Camp, an African policemen, at our request, agreed to telephone people at Cold Comfort Farm to advise them that we had been arrested, and to tell those at Old Umtali and St Augustine Missions that we would come as soon as we were released.

This shows the co-operation of the African people in matters of national importance. Most of the time, for obvious reasons, this co-operation may not be clear, but those of us who have lived for long under the eyes of the police know that it exists, and have often made use of it. The struggle of the African people is one, and where possible all help one another.

Following the successful resistance of the Tangwena people, the Mtema people realised that their problems could be solved in the same way. They sought help from Chief Tangwena, who referred them to us. Their problem was that the government wanted to increase the rentals of the irrigation scheme, which the people had established. They did not agree with the reasons why the Government wanted to raise these rentals. We sought legal advice, and were told that there was

47

nothing that the lawyers could do until an actual case could be brought against them. One of the people in the irrigation area decided to flood-irrigate his land, even though this had been prohibited by the government officials. This man was arrested and taken to Chipinga police camp. Thereupon a message was sent to us, and we travelled with the lawyer to the camp. On arrival we asked to interview the man, and asked the police the section of the Act under which he was being charged. After a short discussion, the prosecutor realised that he had no basis for bringing the case against our man. The charges against him had been brought under a wrong Act, and the Water Rights, under which Act he was charged, were held by a different Government ministry. This showed that those who were complaining against our man had no cause for complaint, and those who should have complained did not do so. On that basis, our man was released. We drove him back to his home at Mtema village, to the great happiness of us and his people, who then continued to use the irrigation water, and encouraged others in the surrounding areas to do the same.

We were aware that this concern for our fellow men would lead us to prison. Hundreds of people who had shown the same concern were locked up in prisons. In Rhodesia prisons are regarded as an institution through which conscientious people will live a part of their lives. St Paul lived a part of his life in prison for preaching the gospel.

4
Prison Life

Sinoia Prison is a Grade III prison more than 70 miles
north of Salisbury. It lies to the south of Sinoia town,
near the railway line which runs between Salisbury
and Sinoia. There was a high fence enclosing the prison
and a big garden, outside of which was a compound
where African warders lived, and two houses where
Jooste and Erasmus lived. The prison buildings behind
a very high wall formed a square. There were two
offices, one where the European officers worked, and
the other was the reception, where the warders received
prisoners and visitors. There were fifteen cells placed
round the square, some being single cells but used to
keep up to three and sometimes six people if they
were not Europeans who required a bed. Cells 1 to 5
had water closets in them, the rest had buckets for
use at night. Cell 10 was for remand prisoners; cell 13
for juveniles in hard labour. Cell 11 was where Walter
Mbambo stayed and I was put in Cell 15. The offices,
cells, kitchen, and toilets were placed in such a way
that the superintendent could observe what was
happening in the garden or in the big courtyard in the
centre of the prison.

During my detention, Mr Henry Jooste was superintendent of the prison. He was a tall thin man, one
month younger than myself. He was born in Rhodesia,

and educated there. His late father had worked at Sinoia in the post office. His mother was still alive and lived in a house in the town which she leased. Henry Jooste was shy, sensitive and quick-tempered. He was chairman of the Sinoia Angler's Club, and his wife was secretary of it for some time. Erasmus was the second-in-command. He was a heavily built man, fond of abusive language and keen to be promoted. He spoke Shona as fluently as he did English and Afrikaans. Both he and Jooste were Afrikaners. Walder was the junior of the three white officers. He was English. He was free and easy with all prisoners, who liked him better than the other two. He was obviously out of place with the two Afrikaners, who did not hesitate to speak in Afrikaans whenever they did not want him to follow their conversation. Walder had worked in the Rhodesian Railways before he joined the prison services, and was obviously more affluent than Jooste and Erasmus.

There were 35 African members of the prison staff. There was one sergeant, four corporals, one lance-corporal, and 29 warders. Sergeant Pasipamire Chisango came from a village about 30 miles south of Salisbury. He was tall, fairly built and very strict. He found it difficult to say the truth about himself and often forgot what he had said when he next talked about the same thing. He had worked in the prisons at Salisbury, Binga and Enkeldoorn before he came to Sinoia in August 1971.

Corporal Edward Chiwunye came from St Albert's Mission, which is near Mount Darwin. He was as old as I was. He went to school up to Standard Five (to the age of fourteen for an African, nine for a European child) and then decided to find work at Bulawayo. For a year he was unemployed and was very happy when he was offered a job as a warder, which he has done since 1958. He boasts about escorting President Kaunda to and from Northern Rhodesia when the president was in Salisbury Prison. Edward was trusted by Jooste, which made him untrusted by his African mates.

Corporal Dzingai Zimuto worked in the army prior to joining the prison service. He had quite a lot to say about his stay in Malaya, some of which we were told to take with a grain of salt. He put his own version to every story he told. During his life he had contracted sleeping sickness. When he was not yarning a long story he would stand facing the wall and doze or sit at a bench with his back towards the superintendent's window. He always sat with his belt in his hands, so that if the superintendent came up to him during his sleep he would stand up and pretend to have been wide awake, and put on his belt. If a prisoner came to tease him during his periods of dozing he would wallop him with his belt. He was most entertaining.

Corporal Funda had his home in Zambia. He was born in 1934 and came to Rhodesia to work in the wattle plantations. He then joined the prison services and worked at a number of places before he was stationed at Sinoia. He is of the Lozi tribe: very perticular about his appearance, and very careful about his rights, he was proud of them too. He would be better off working in the Zambian prison service, a thing we often reminded him of, but he wanted to qualify for a gratuity in the Rhodesian services so that he could go back to Zambia where he hoped to support a wife and three children on it.

Corporal Mudondo came from the Charter District from a place called Nharira. He had a wife and two young children. He was quite elderly—it was difficult to estimate his age—but very pleasant. He was the most pleasant corporal that we found in Sinoia Prison: very kind and very sympathetic.

Of the junior staff, Robert Mabika was the most responsible. He worked in the reception with Chiwanga, and he was a good example of a young African. He knew that what he was doing was wrong, but thought that his services would be required by any future African government. He was about the same age as Walter Mbambo, who was being detained for his wish for the freedom of his countrymen. Mabika had passed a test to become a corporal, as it meant more cash. He was in the process of getting married, and could hardly face life in the same manner as Walter and I. He respected our feelings and respected our outlook, but thought that as long as he was employed he would be a yes-man. Chiwanga was much younger than Mbambo, very full of himself, and on occasions he thought he was the owner of the prison. He was very cruel to the hard labour prisoners, and for that reason we could not get on well together.

In the prison all the prisoners were classified according to their offence and conduct. There were four classes—A, B, C, and D. There were two class A prisoners, Sarikosi and Duncan. Duncan was a pleasant man; light in complexion and about 5 feet 3 inches tall. He knew a lot of trades, which he did to the pleasure of all. He was a motor mechanic by profession. His carpentry was good, and he could make perfect sandals from a motor car's tyres. He was very good at languages and could speak five quite fluently. Before he was imprisoned, he worked as a farm manager. The farm owner did not live on his farm. Duncan sold the

cattle and kept the money for himself. For this offence
he had to serve three years hard labour.

Class A prisoners were left to work on their own:
they could go in and out of the fence and gates without escort. Sarikosi worked in the office and made tea
for the officers, and brought in food, for the white
prisoners, which was prepared at the Superintendent's
house.

Class B prisoners worked in gangs and each gang was
watched by a warder, who carried a gun and a truncheon.
These prisoners could leave the fence and go to work
digging trenches, loading and unloading railway trucks,
digging graves and burying unclaimed bodies. From this
class was chosen those prisoners who cooked our meals
and did the laundry.

Class C consisted of prisoners who could not leave
the fence surrounding the prison.

Class D was composed of dangerous prisoners such
as armed robbers. All people convicted of political
offences were automatically placed in this class. Walter
Mbambo and I were put in that class although we were
detainees and not criminals.

There were not more than 200 prisoners at the prison
at any one time. I was the 1,678th prisoner to be
admitted into Sinoia Prison by November 1970. I spent
a total of 741 days in prison, 477 of these days being
spent in Sinoia Prison of which 250 days were in
solitary confinement. I was then transferred to Salisbury
Prison where I lived for 264 days with ZANU friends.
I was taken twice to Salisbury to appear before the
Review Tribunal; later I went to Sinoia police station
to be interrogated, first by the chief superintendent
of the Mashonaland North Security Police, and subsequently by an inspector of the security police, of

the same area. What joy we had when Walter Mbambo and I were allowed on 4 August 1971, after nine months of separation, to speak to each other! Gertrude's and other friends' visits to the prison also brought with it a change in the routine.

On any one routine day, my clothes were taken away from me every night, so they had to be brought to me each morning. After dressing I emptied my bucket into the toilet and cleaned it. I washed myself and then did muscle exercises. After that I cleaned my cell. Breakfast was brought at 8.30 a.m. It was brought in three bowls by two hard labour prisoners, under the escort of warders, and placed on the floor from which I ate it. In one bowl there was hard cooked *sadza*. In another black un-sugared coffee, and in the third there was clean drinking water. Two hard labour prisoners and warders carrying truncheons came to collect the utensils after I had eaten.

My cell was number 15 and was 8 feet by 6 feet; it opened into a courtyard 16 feet square with barbed wire on top. From the courtyard one could go into the toilet and shower room. I was locked up in this courtyard while I was having a shower, and this took place on every morning of the 250 days, solitary confinement that I spent in this place. During this time I squatted in the corner of the courtyard sometimes, and read the Bible for a couple of hours, and did the *surya namaskas* an Indian relaxation exercise for thirty minutes, or I walked round the cell. At 11.30 the warders and hard labour prisoners brought the next meal of the day. This was *sadza* with *nyemba*. The plates were left in the courtyard and collected after the last meal of the day. After the meal at 11.30 I was locked up from 12 p.m. to 1.30 p.m. In the winter it was too cold to fall asleep, but in spring and summer the concrete floor had a cooling effect and I occasionally fell asleep. At 2.30 I took another shower and read the Bible before the final meal of the day was brought at 3 p.m. Then my cell was locked up until the following morning.

For the others, every day started with the parade of the warders at 6 a.m. conducted by one of the corporal warders and followed by an inspection by the sergeant. This took place in the presence of one of the white prison officials, who would have opened the armoury where the warders' guns and ammunition were kept. While the parade and inspection were in progress, one corporal warder and two warders unlocked the cells and counted the prisoners in each cell, checking the number against that of the previous night. The prisoners washed using water in cups which they brought from the tap at the side of the kitchen. Those who used buckets as toilets during the night emptied and cleaned the buckets at the same time. By 6.30 a.m. all the hard labour prisoners would have had their breakfast of black un-sugared coffee and *sadza*. They were arranged into gangs ready for a sort of roll call as each gang went out to do the mornings work. Each armed warder was ready outside the wall of the prison to take his gang out. This was done by 7 a.m. The white officer in charge of unlocking went back home, probably to have his breakfast.

The warders in the reception called into their office all new arrivals to check their belongings in, and those finishing their terms of imprisonment to check them out. Those prisoners on remand and custody who were going to appear before the court were given their uniforms and stood in a line at the gate. At 7.30 a.m. the other two white officers arrived. They looked round the place to make sure that all was in order. If there was a white prisoner to take to court they dealt with him. Of the corporals, one went to Sinoia court; the second travelled to places near Sinoia where periodical courts were held; the third worked in the garden within the fence surrounding the prison, and checked the visitors in and out of the prison; and the fourth worked in the courtyard in charge of gangs that cleaned the cells and cooked our meals, and of the remand prisoners and two detainees.

Corporal Dzingai was doing this duty the day I was detained. On 19 November 1970, after all that is described above had been done, he and two others came to my cell and unlocked it. The doors of all the cells opened outwards. He stood holding the door, looking frightened. I was still naked. He asked one of the warders to fetch a khaki prison uniform for me. He asked me what was wrong with me, and I told him nothing. 'Then why are you here?' he asked. I told him that I didn't know. The warder brought the uniform, and I put it on. All three men led me to the reception. To get there I had to pass through a metal gate which was attended to by a warder all the time. The door which led into the reception room was locked after I got in. There were expressions of fear on everyone's faces. Erasmus was in the white officers' room further along; he came into the reception room and ordered me to stand up straight. I looked straight into his eyes without changing my position. Then he turned to one of the warders and ordered him to tell me to stand up straight. The warder told Erasmus that I understood English. He said that that did not matter: the warder should tell me to stand up straight. Still I did

not change the position in which I was standing.
Erasmus then asked who I was and I told him. Then he
said, pointing to the warder, 'That boy will make a
record of your belongings and yourself.'

The 'boy' Mabika, was 24 years old. I thought he
would protest. He did not. I was too angry to protest.
For a moment I thought Mabika was not one of us.
I felt angry that he did not defend his manhood. Then
I asked how old he was. He said 24 years. 'Then you
are not a boy', I told him. Mabika did not say anything.
I had asked him in Shona, not knowing that Erasmus
understood and spoke Shone fluently. Mabika did not
answer, because he agreed with me, but did not want
to contradict his boss.

The boss turned to me to confirm that Mabika was
a boy. He said to me in Shona, 'He knows that he is a
boy.'

'Rubbish', I said.

Mabika looked at me admiringly, and Erasmus went
out of the room.

Then in Shona Mabika said 'What is your name, old
man?'

'Didymus,' I said.

'Your address?'

'Cold Comfort Farm.'

'Your offence?'

'I don't know.'

Mabika said, 'It is law and order.'

I said, 'What do you mean?'

Mabika said, 'It means you are being detained under
the law and order maintenance regulations.' Then he
asked me what my Registration Certificate (R.C.)
number was. I told him it was X 24873 Makoni.

'Who is your chief?' I told him it was Makoni.

'Your headman?' I said 'Mutasa'.

'Your tribe?' I told him 'Muwungwe'.

'Your religion?'

I said 'Leave it blank.'

'Don't you belong to any church?'

I said I did but that I did not want it to be written down. Then finally, after thinking, I told him I was an Anglican.

Then he said 'Will you show me what is in that suitcase?'

I showed him everything, item by item, from my handkerchief, pair of shoes, pair of socks, to a jacket and radio. He told me that I was not allowed to keep the radio, my wristwatch, or any of the clothes that I had brought with me.

Then the door was opened and a white doctor, Dr Bingham, came in followed by Sarikosi carrying a tray on which was a teapot and cups. The doctor glanced at me and went into the white officers' room. Jooste and Walder had come in earlier. After Mabika had made his record he ushered me into the officers' room. Each of the three officers were sitting behind a desk, holding a cup of tea. The doctor sat in an easy chair and said 'He is allright.' Jooste was about to introduce the doctor, but kept quiet after what the doctor had said. I was ushered out of the room, and out of the reception room; the three warders, in the end, came to the gate and led me to Cell 15, where I spent most of my time.

Various people came into Sinoia Prison between 9 a.m. and 11.30 a.m. to see their relatives, friends, bosses, or servants. Some were treated carelessly, and others very well. At 12 noon the gangs were brought back to the prison for the mid-day meal. They were taken out again at 1 p.m. At this time the white officers went to feed and rest until 2 p.m. By 3.30 p.m. all the remand prisoners would have had showers and fed. They were locked up at 4, when the gangs came in to feed.

Before they fed they came into the yard through the steel gate, stripped naked and handed their prison uniforms to warders who felt them to see if there was anything in them that could be used to break out or harm other prisoners. The prisoners were told to jump up and clap their hands above their heads and throw their legs apart. If anything harmful was between their legs or under their armpits it would fall. The prisoners carried their uniforms to the shower, where they put themselves under the shower. They were not provided with towels to dry themselves after the shower so many of them put on their clothes whilst their bodies were still wet. In winter many used to shiver during their supper which was brought immediately after the shower. After supper all prisoners lined up at the door of their cells and were counted as they went into their cells. They would be searched for a second time before they went in. This was lock-up time. If the number of prisoners was the one shown on the board in the officers' room, all was well. The cells were locked, and the keys put into a safe until the following morning. The warders who kept watch during the night locked up under the supervision of one of the corporals.

When the warders at Sinoia had caught up with who I was and why I was detained, they gossiped about how I used to answer back to their bosses. The night warders used to take turns to come to talk to me between 6 p.m. and 8 p.m. They kept me up to date with news and what was going on at the prison. They told me of the banning of the Cold Comfort Farm Society. After this I realised that I was not alone. The conscience of our people was one. We only came to a turning point at different times. And the speed of coming to this turning point was increasing, and is going to increase.

The daily routine at Sinoia Prison used to be broken by Gertrude's visit. It was a great event for me every week. Something told me she was coming; this was confirmed by the warder's footsteps towards my cell, the jingle of the keys, and the words 'You have a visitor—your wife.' I was led to the steel gates as usual and into the reception room where I stood on one side of the iron bars across the windows, and spoke to Gertrude standing on the other side. She was usually allowed to bring one other visitor. Before Guy and Molly Clutton-Brock were compelled to leave the country, they always came with her; at other times it was Gertrude's closest friends and our friends at Cold Comfort Farm before it was closed.

On my side of the bars I stood under guard of an African warder, and if there was a European visitor, the European warder would be there too. On the other side there was Gertrude and an African security police-man or a white one if a European friend was visiting me. Every time that Gertrude came, she brought food to supplement my prison rations. At first she had to test all the food that she brought and could not leave any bottled food. After protest this was discontinued.

Following further protests, our visit was allowed to take place in the officers' room sitting on chairs. Our lawyer, who had much to do with this improvement wrote: 'Thank you very much for your letter of 8th September. I enclose for your information a copy of a letter I have submitted to the tribunal. I have also written to the prison superintendent of Sinoia, asking (a) for Gertrude's visits to be extended to an hour, (b) for all letters to you from Gertrude to be handed to you in the normal way, (c) that you be permitted to discuss matters with her in Shona.'

At the end of the period of my solitary confinement, I was allowed to spend the time between 8 p.m. and 3.30 p.m. with Walter Mbambo in the main courtyard. As he is still in detention it would not be proper to say a lot about him, other than that he appeared in court before Judge Dandy Young, who sentenced him to ten years' imprisonment, seven of which were suspended for three years. After serving his three-year sentence of hard labour at Khami prison, Walter was detained at Sinoia Prison at the end of September 1970. He was 29 years old. His father fought during the Second World War and at the end of it was given a job as a messenger under the District Commissioner. This was his father's reward for fighting during the Second World War. After his father's death, Walter's mother worked very hard to bring Walter up. She is now living in Salisbury and visited Walter as often as she could, at Sinoia Prison.

I was brought from Sinoia Prison to Salisbury Prison on 8 March 1972. The routine at Salisbury Prison was very different from that at Sinoia. The relationship between the superintendent and the detainees was appalling. I discovered this when I talked to the superintendent before I was taken to the detainees' section of Salisbury Remand Prison.

The Superintendent told me very briefly what went on at the prison, and then indicated that there was a disagreement, an intense one, as he said, between himself and the detainees. Then he asked me if I could decide on whose side I wanted to be. As a detainee it was quite clear on whose side I was to be. The detainees had been moved from the top floor of one block of the prison building to a section where European and coloured remand prisoners used to be kept. Each detainee had a room to himself and shared a yard with two others. I shared such a yard with Robert Mugabe and Morton Malianga.

Robert Mugabe is the general secretary of ZANU. He used to address many meetings at Highfield and Harare at which many people were present. It was obvious why so many people liked to hear him. He is a grey haired man, nearing 50 years old, and quietly spoken. We called him Va Gushungu or Bob, a sign of affection which was well deserved. Robert has a good sense of humour, very high principles and discipline; his clarity of speech and thought demonstrates his determination to serve his people. This has led him to his present period of detention which has lasted since 1964. After staying with him for eight months and listening very carefully to his wise counsel and decisions he impressed me as one of our best leaders. He obtained a Master's Degree in Education and one in Law, and is working for a Doctorate in Education. There was no question that our well-being as a group depended very much on Robert's leadership. He acted very quickly whenever the group's interests were threatened. For this he got the support of the group. When the group discussed any matter, Robert listened most of the time, which gave him the opportunity to make sound decisions and to help the group along during the most trying periods of our lives.

5
A Day in Prison: Thoughts

My thoughts centred around the illegal regime, and
those aiding it. I considered the illegal Rhodesian
government was like a gang of armed robbers, with its
servants as accomplices. They have no right to exercise
power or authority in Rhodesia except with the consent
of the majority of the inhabitants of the country, who
are at this moment black. After UDI that power and
authority has been used to rob the rights of black
people of our country.

When those who came to arrest me disclosed their
intention, I thought I would spend most of my time
discussing with other prisoners my thoughts and theirs.
I thought that in this way I would remain active in the
struggle for the freedom of our people. This hope disappeared when I discovered that I was kept away from
the other prisoners. I wondered whether the security
police thought that I would influence them. This
reminded me that on 17 July 1970 Mr W.H.H. Nicolle,
the then Secretary of Internal Affairs, had written to
me as follows:

To: Dydymus Noel Edwin Mutasa (X 24783 Makoni)

**NOTICE IN TERMS OF SECTION 45 (4) (b)
OF THE AFRICAN AFFAIRS ACT (Chapter 92)**

(1) Take notice that under the provisions of paragraph (b)

63

of subsection (4) of section 45 of the African Affairs Act (Chapter 92), I do hereby prohibit you from entering or remaining in any Tribal Trust Land in Rhodesia.

(2) Failure to comply with this notice renders you liable to prosecution. The notice will remain in force until it is revoked.

W. H. H. NICOLLE
Secretary for Internal Affairs

Section 45 4(b) of the African Affairs Act states that:

'Notwithstanding the provision of subsection 1 of section 2, any person may be prohibited from entering or remaining in any Tribal Trust Land, or other tribal area, by written notice by the Secretary of Internal Affairs, after full inquiry by him, if the Minister or the Secretary for Internal Affairs, as the case may be, is of the opinion that the presence of such a person in such tribal trust land or area is undesirable in the public interest of the Africans living in such tribal trust land or area.'

What was it that I had done which was not 'in the interest' of our people? Just as it was undesirable for me to remain with our people in the Tribal Trust Land, it was found undesirable that I should live with other prisoners for the first nine months of my detention. The question cropped up quite often in my mind until Cold Comfort Farm was declared an unlawful organisation. Then it appeared to me that, as it was impossible for me 'to enter or remain in any Tribal Trust Land', I could not remain in an European area following the ban of the Cold Comfort Farm Society. The reasoning of the Security Police was that I could, therefore, only remain in prison. Having clarified this point in my mind, I prepared myself to remain in prison, for as long as the

Rhodesian Front was in power.

Then my thoughts would turn to Gertrude and the children. I was of the opinion that the Rhodesian Front illegal government would remain in power up to 1975. So I prepared myself to stay in prison till then, but I was not quite sure whether Gertrude would be prepared to wait for me all that time. Arrangements had been made for the provision of her material needs and those of the children through HEKS, the relief fund of the Federation of Swiss Protestant Churches. We had discussed this with Guy Clutton-Brock and were quite satisfied for all we knew, then. Gertrude was happy about this arrangement but obviously unhappy to be alone. There was nothing she could do against this situation. I thought she could do what she liked if she found the situation unbearable. My first letter to her was as follows:- 'I should have written earlier but circumstances did not permit. I am allowed one letter a week, in and out. I had not seen a prison cell before though I visited many friends lingering in them. Now I come face to face with one. I do not know whether it is allowed to write about it, but one day I shall tell you all about it. My spirit is high.'

In other letters I tried to let her know what was happening, without risking their delivery to her.

1/1/72 ... 'As you may be expecting I must tell you about my reading of *The Gospel of St Luke* by William Burclay. It will be too long for me to relate remarks which are made in connection with the following quotations, but all the same they will bear quite a lot of meaning to you. Maybe the same as they do to me: "The challenge from the Beatitudes is: will you be happy in the world's way or in Christ's way? To take up the Cross, meant to be prepared to face things like that 2,000 rebels were crucified on crosses which were set in line along the roadside, so that they made a dreadful warning to others for loyalty to God. It means to be ready to endure the worst that men can do to us for the sake of being true to God. Christianity does not mean knowing about Christ. It means knowing Christ. It is the task of Christianity to make not new things, but new men; and once the new men are created a new world will surely follow. That is why the church is the most important institution in the world for it is the factory where men are produced. There are those who seem to think that just because they are members of a Christian civilisation, all is well. They would differentiate between themselves and the poor heathen, in their ignorance and in their blindness. But he who lives in a Christian civilisation is not necessarily a Christian. He may be enjoying all its benefits; he is certainly living on Christian capital which others before him have built up, but it is no reason for sitting back content and sure that all is well. It is a challenge which asks us; what did you do to initiate all this? What have you done to preserve and develop it? We cannot live on borrowed goodness. The individual Christian must be the conscience of the nation. The Church must be such that she speaks fearlessly, against all evil, and supports fearlessly all good causes. She must be such that she will never hold her peace through fear, or favour of man.

4/12/70 ... 'There is a very special chorus which is always my heart-soother whenever I begin to worry: "I know who holds my future and I know He holds my hand. With God things don't just happen. Everything by Him is planned. And as I face tomorrow with its problems, great and small, I will trust the God of miracles. Give him my all." '

9/12/70 ... 'Prison life is such a funny thing which frightens one at first but gets into one's veins as time goes on. Then, I think, prison loses its corrective function.'

'Mind you, this is the first time that I have been in prison. But if I were a "loafer" with nothing to do, I would be thinking that all my troubles are solved.'

18/1/71 ... 'You said you did not know whether you should be bitter. My most sincere advice is that you should never be bitter about anything. It is wrong to be bitter. The whole thing is a "cup" and we have got to accept it because we are not in a position to change it. We are not in a position to judge anybody either because God is the only one capable of doing that. Please learn to take things as they are. I know you are anxious to be with me but there is nothing we can do now to make it so.'

8/3/71 ... 'How much does one have to grow spiritually? One is always put in a position where one has to pardon even when the wrong is done to oneself or one's friends. For example, an African warder came back from leave and one of the prisoners extended his hand to greet the warder. The warder extended his foot and kicked the prisoner's hand. Would you feel sorry for the prisoner or for the warder?'

6/12/71 ... 'I am not so lonely. I have acquired a new friend, the spider, which keeps company with me, and is very kind to me. It is making its net round the room to catch the mosquitos which bite me at night.

'... you talk about good food. I think of it in terms of Guy's prayer before our meals at Cold Comfort Farm. You remember he used to pray, "Bless oh Lord this food to our use and us to Thy service." I say the same prayer for the horrible food we eat here. Actually the prayer reminds me of Guy. I shall always remember him by it; not because I am of any service to God here! ... But who knows ... I may be.'

It was important to think about the Church, because almost every African in Rhodesia belongs to one denomination of the Church or another. Those leading in the liberation of our people, bear such names as George, Robert, Edward, Herbert. These people are Christians, and so are their ideals.

Through Cold Comfort Farm we have established very good contact with Cristian schools and other institutions. All the young people of these institutions had different views about the role of the Church in Rhodesia. Many were disappointed with this role of the Church, and so was I. But I attended a Christian service at Mufakose. The sermon was given by a young man training to be a priest. During the sermon, he made references to 'our brothers fighting in the Zambezi valley'. He asked us to pray for them. It reminded me of what I had heard about the Reverend Caanan Banana before he was vice-president of the African National Council. The Christian Council of Rhodesia was considering sending chaplains to the Rhodesian armed forces. The Reverend Cannan Banana suggested that this would be wrong, unless similar chaplains were sent to the freedom fighters.

At the present moment there are army- as well as prison-chaplains provided by the Christian Council of Rhodesia to serve the illegal regime. On 21 July 1973, *Moto,* the Roman Catholic newspaper which is read mostly by Africans, reported that 'an Essexvale man, Corporal Shadreck, who had joined the Rhodesian African Rifles in 1963, shortly before UDI, was given a military funeral at Matthew Barracks last week. Leading the funeral service, attended by hundreds of people including Corporal Shadreck's father, was Major the Reverend D.W.R. Bird of the First Battalion, who was assisted by three other ministers.'

It is known that the World Council of Churches aids the liberation movements in southern Africa. But to our knowledge, no World Council of Churches funds have been transmitted to the liberation movements through the Christian Council of Rhodesia. Any funds that have been given by the World Council of Churches, have been for the Council to use for church work in Rhodesia. The Rhodesia Council of Churches has been most critical of the World Council of Churches' aid to the liberation movements in southern Africa, but have not taken into account the services that Rhodesian clergymen are rendering to the illegal regime.

At Cold Comfort Farm Society we received a grant through the Christian Council of Rhodesia, to buy land in Rhodesia. The grant was made in 1967, well before the decision of the World Council of Churches' programme to combat racism was made in 1970. The Cold Comfort Farm Society was banned because it was suspected of aiding freedom fighters, but the Christian Council of Rhodesia, through which the grant was made, still exists and functions in Rhodesia. Was Cold Comfort Farm Society banned because it was championing the cause of our people more than the Church?

During the first week of my stay in Sinoia Prison after I had been told that I was considered the most dangerous person in the prison, an Anglican priest came to see me. He was allowed into the cell, and a chair was brought in for him. I sat on the toilet bucket, which I used at night, and tried to discover why he had been let in. He told me that he came from Salisbury at the request of the Bishop of Mashonaland. For a moment I wondered whether he was a Security Policeman dressed in a clergyman's clothes. I told him, as we discussed a number of things, that I would be appearing before the Review Tribunal, but that I would never accept the illegal regime as the lawful government of my country.

'Do you want to stay in this place for ever?' he asked. 'I have no choice,' I said.

'My advice is that you should accept these people as the government if you want to be released. You have got to be as wise as a serpent, and as harmless as a dove.'

I had given the same advice to many of the young people that I knew. On this occasion I thought the advice was out of place. I never accepted it.

The next time that the same priest visited the prison, he was dressed in prison uniform, much better than that of the Superintendent. He was the senior prison chaplain. I thought I was wise not to have told him much about myself.

Apart from the Reverend Clark, who was the senior chaplain of the prison services, I came across four other prison chaplains, or padres as they were called. Two of them were white and two were Africans. The Rev. Swift and Rev. Rebeiro were Roman Catholic priests. Father Swift was of retiring age but decided to continue to work in the prison services. Robert Mugabe used to tell me that I had to tell Father Swift the same thing over and over again, every time that he came to see us, before he could remember to do it. White padres were allowed to bring, or take away from us, what they might. The same did not apply to African padres. They

70

had to disclose what they were taking into or out of the prison. In fact, although they were priests, and equal with other priests in the sight of God, they were not regarded as such in the prison

The position of the Rhodesian churches towards the illegal regime is not explicit, but they seem friendly. Church leaders have dined with ministers of the illegal regime or invited them to address their congregations, saying that they must maintain contact with the government, but this contact has developed into friendship and a disregard of evil. As the Church's teaching is quite clear about evil, it is not right that it should condone evil, and particularly that which is being created by the present illegal regime, since the declaration of illegal independence. This evil will never be forgotten by the Africans, no matter how clergymen may like to sweep it under the carpet.

When we learnt of agreement which had been reached between the British Government and the illegal regime, contained in the proposals for a settlement which were published in 1971, my thoughts turned to this fact. The proposals did not seek to remove the evil that exists in Rhodesian society but, like the churches, just to sweep the evil under the carpet. Until that evil is uprooted, there can be no stability in Rhodesia. In discussion with Sir Glyn Jones, one of the Commissioners investigating the acceptability of the 1971 proposals, Walter Mbambo and I made the following views known to him.

1. There was fear and unwillingness on the part of the illegal regime to follow the spirit of the 1961 Constitution, which the regime disliked 'because it advanced the Africans too rapidly.' This unwillingness and fear led to the illegal declaration of independence and the

the break down of Anglo-Rhodesian relations in 1965.
Nothing has happened to show that different attitudes
or values have been adopted by the illegal regime.

2. The proposals should be rejected, on the gounds
that the Africans want a greater say and participation
in the running of their country than is offered to them
in the proposals. The reasons for rejecting the 1961
Constitution was the desire by the illegal regime to
implement a policy of separate development. The con-
sequence of this desire was the detention of innocent
people without trial, and the illegal declaration of
independence. These were calculated efforts by the
illegal regime to suppress the African population. These
efforts have been counteracted by successful guerrilla
warfare which is threatening the internal security of
the country. Any worthwhile agreement should be
between the leaders of the Liberation Movement and
the regime.

3. The agreement between Her Majesty's Government
and the illegal regime which contained the proposals
for the settlement, is seen by us as a measure by Her
Majesty's Government to save the illegal regime from
the consequences and failure of UDI and as a guaran-
tee by the British government of its interests in this
country.

4. Immediately after the illegal Declaration of Independence, the failure of Her Majesty's Government to
send a police force to restore law and order in the
colony was deplored. Her Majesty's Government stated
that it would intervene when there was a break-down of
law and order. During your presence thirteen Africans
were shot dead by the Rhodesian security forces of the
illegal regime but, as if this was not loss of blood, no
protest is made by the British Government. Now that

a determined effort is being made by Africans to defend their rights, they are coerced into accepting the continuation of an illegal government, by the fact that if they don't accept the proposals, Her Majesty's Government would abandon its responsibilities to the people of Rhodesia, and would not continue to seek a formula of government which is acceptable to the people of Rhodesia as a whole. We reject the proposals because they encourage the continuation of the present bad government; they are coercive and dishonourable.

5. Other reasons why the proposals should be rejected are: the inability of Her Majesty's Government to consult at all with the African population or its leaders, only requiring them to say yes or no in a matter of such vital importance to the African population. in setting up the proposals which reflect and endorse the views of the illegal regime, Her Majesty's Government is clearly siding with that regime. This makes Africans suspicious and dissatisfied with the role of Her Majesty's Government, with its intention and responsibility towards the African population whom it should have been representing during the talks for a settlement.

6. During the last ten years the Rhodesian population has been encouraged by the illegal regime to believe that separate development was the only answer to the country's problems. No convincing reason has yet been advanced by that regime (the Rhodesia Front) why this policy should be sacrificed in favour of independence. There is nothing in the proposals to prevent the policy of separate development from being re-implemented after legal independence has been conferred on Rhodesia. We knew all along that separate development is ruinous to race relations and the future of this country; but we are not convinced that the present illegal regime

73

believes the same. If it does, what is there at present
to stop it from implementing the principles of democracy? And why does it have to seek recognition of its
independence through a set of proposals which do not
involve our leaders or include the wishes of the majority
of the people?

7. In accepting the proposals for a settlement the illegal
regime was hoping to escape from a situation which it
created. The proposals seek to reward the illegal regime
for its mistakes. This is a price, bordering on insult,
too dear for the Africans to give to the illegal regime.

8. A change of heart made by the illegal regime will be
accepted by the Africans when there is a genuine reconciliation which buries all differences and corrects
the mistakes which have been made by the illegal regime.
We believe that this will only come about when there
is a popular government elected by the majority of the
population.

9. The proposals to grant independence to a minority
regime is therefore most alarming. The African population has been misgoverned for the last eighty years,
and more so during the last six years. Good faith
requires that the bad laws under which Africans are
misgoverned should be changed before independence
is granted. No fool would be persuaded to give up the
little that they have in order to be given a lot which
does not exist. To require that this should be so is
putting the cart before the horse, and deserves the
answer 'no'.

Many other detainees gave their views about the
1971 settlement proposals. In their report, the Pearce
Commissioners noted: 'We met the 63 detainees either
individually or in small groups. On each occasion a
memorandum, usually lengthy, representing the views

of the group was first read out. Then each individual
added his own additional reasons for rejecting the
proposals. As one would expect from people who have
had ample opportunity to brood on what they regard
as the injustices of the society in which they live, the
detainees spoke both passionately and emphatically.
Many of them revealed a good, if indirect knowledge
of events in Rhodesia, and had a firm grasp of the
proposals.' The Commissioners attached as an example
of the documents submitted, a memorandum by Mr
Joshua Nkomo and their report continues: 'He told us
that he had hoped that a settlement would give him
his freedom. It was therefore difficult for him to say
"No" when this meant that he might be committing
himself to another ten years of detention, but he considered that he had no alternative.

'The detainees were unanimous in denouncing the
proposals, and claimed that rejection offered the only
hope for ultimate African progress. They produced
closely reasoned criticism of every aspect of the proposals. In the main, they were uncompromising in
their demand for immediate majority rule. Some im-
plied that if their demands were not met, violence
would inevitably ensue.

"We need no sympathy, we only want fair play and
justice. If Britain abandons us to ourselves, then it is
we ourselves who will defend our rights. In time we
should take back our country, even at the cost of our
lives."

'But they showed little bitterness towards Europeans
as such. Only towards the Rhodesian government. All
speakers displayed a deep and total distrust of them:
"independence under this government is unthinkable."
They were also dismayed that the British government

should appear to be willing to forgive rather than punish the rebels (a word frequently used). The failure to secure the release of all detainees and to ensure that the African Nationalist leaders were properly consulted, was also emphasised. "Sir Alec knows who the leaders of the African people are but despite that he decides to leave them in oblivion." One criticism made by many of the detainees in particular, though we also heard it from others, was the failure of the proposals to provide any safeguard for those now under sentence of death for their activities against the Rhodesian authorities since UDI.

'Nevertheless, given their predicament, many showed a remarkable tolerance and readiness to think constructively. They asked that there should be genuine consultations between all races, and several argued that there should be some form of constitutional conference under Britian's independent chairmanship.'

When I was transferred from Sinoia to Salisbury Prison in March 1972, we were thinking much of the outcome of the proposals and the verdict of the Pearce Commissioners. There was no doubt in our minds that if the verdict was 'yes' there would be a lot of trouble. But that if it was 'no' there would be some time for reflection.

We had also, of course, to think about the future of our country. These thoughts centred on the young people because they would have much more of that future to cope with than us. From our experience at Cold Comfort Farm Society, we know of the desire of young people to live freely, and that with guidance they can live constructively. The young people of Cold Comfort Farm showed this and they lived unselfishly finding their livelihood from the land.

Based on the present population figures of Rhodesia, our land resources can support more than twice the present population. In 1971 there were 637,000 African children in primary schools, 26,183 children in secondary schools, 2,024 in Teacher Training Colleges and 937 at the University College of Rhodesia. This is a total of 666,144 young people at school. If half of the 5½ million Africans are young, there must be nearly 2 million young people who are not at school. There were 775,800 Africans employed in that year. Assuming that all employed are young (which is not the case), there must be at least nearly 1 million young people not doing anything in Rhodesia. It is known that many who left school failed to find employment. Opportunities could be found if schemes such as the Cold Comfort Farm Scoiety were encouraged. Not only would the young people find employment, but they would learn to take responsibility and to determine their own future. A lot of the land which is lying idle in the 'European areas' could be used economically for the benefit of the country rather than used as speculations by the capitalists.

People, not only in Rhodesia, require a classless society. This cannot be achieved by talking about it alone; but also by practising it in living in our country. Young people have got to learn here and now that freedom is not to do what they want to, but to do what is right: and to do what is right in Rhodesia means making use of the available resources, which at present are land and labour, in order to raise the standard of living of all the people. Many people think that the standard of living can be raised if their children are sent to school. Those who have been to school think that they then acquire a right to a higher standard of living, having had so much public money spent on them during their education. They expect higher salaries than those who were not educated, instead of requiring less because they are better equipped to get on in life than the less educated. They should regard their employment as an opportunity of returning to the nation the investment made on them. They should do this by giving faithful service to the country and working in undertakings that give the maximum returns to the nation.

Our country has been greatly exploited by capitalists. Up to now these capitalists have been mostly white. Politicians in Rhodesia, and particularly the young people, must guard against them, if only to avoid having to get rid of them in the future.

Young people also require a united world. Those in Rhodesia must first achieve their liberation before they can be accepted as equals by the rest of the young people of the world. It is only on this basis that they can value their unity. Only then will they be able to hold their heads up high. Otherwise they can only live as beggars in their own country and in the world. Every parent should show love to their children, by showing them the way to earn self-confidence with which they can face the future.

We discussed the ideals of sharing knowledge and other resources, human or natural. There is yet much for our 'educated' people to learn about this. We hope that those of us who take a lead in the defence of our people's rights can consolidate this insight into our people's minds by setting an example. Rhodesian detainees are in the best position to demonstrate this type of simple living. It is practised by most people living in Rhodesia. Detainees have been deprived of the means to make a better living. It is hoped that they will not feel that they have got to make up for their deprivation, but that they would use their position to encourage their people to live simply until the country can provide a decent living for everybody. If good living cannot be provided for all it may not be provided for a few. It should be remembered that the opportunity lost by the detainees, through no fault of theirs, is also being lost by the majority of the people through expoitation of one form or another.

African political leaders are campaigning against the Smith regime with the support of the people. They stand the risk of being rejected by their people as 'black Smiths', if they seek to replace the present illegal regime without changing many aspects of the present Rhodesian way of life. Those who are supporting these leaders could then justifiably reject them just as they are rejecting the Smith regime. There is no doubt that the present illegal regime will come to an end within a short time. When the time comes, we hope our people would know the type of future which is desirable for all the people of Rhodesia. It is also hoped that those who have been lucky enough to go to universities, or other institutions of higher learning, will help their people to make a correct assessment of the problems that will lie ahead of them in a free country. This involves selfless leadership, and the co-operation of all involved in that future.

It was very simple to think of our oppression when we lived at Sinoia Prison. At any one time there were over 200 black people, and only 3 white ones. Of the black, 35 helped to maintain the oppressors' position. When discussing this with some of the African warders I realised that an immense amount of work will have to be done to make some of our people conscious of their rights and how to obtain them.

There is no short cut; only a long time of educative effort can make our people conscious of the strong position that they hold. Our people are in an apparently weak position, not because there is little money in our country, but because what money there is is used by the regime to make some people believe that only by doing jobs such as warders, security-policemen or soldiers can they share in that money. The same attitude can be seen in many of our Rhodesian intellectuals or academics who are knocking around Britain, acquiring higher and higher education in the hope of fitting themselves better into the exploitive society. Those in Britain should be in a better position to organise and to formulate helpful ideas about the liberation of our country; instead many engage in fruitless arguments about who will be the leader. Surely there cannot be a leader until the country and people are free. As long as we expect other people to free the country for us, we have no right to say who will lead them.

The present situation in our country can therefore not be blamed entirely upon the wickedness of the white people; those of us who are not prepared to risk our future so that our people make use of their strong position are also to be blamed. Our people should be made conscious of the fact that the white society is able to maintain itself only by making use of us. The illegal regime would have been toppled if Africans had withdrawn their labour. There would have been no need for sanctions or help from anywhere. It may not be too late for our people to think quite seriously about taking such an action.

6
The Struggle

Lord Acton's dictum, 'Power tends to corrupt' seems to particularly fit with British imperialism in Rhodesia where we see the story of a powerful nation in relation to a weak people. One must confess that there have been elements of deception and chicanery in that relationship. Before imperial colonialism, countries like China, India, Persia, and Egypt had flourishing civilisations. Their cultural patterns ensured the continuation of these forms of civilisation. After the conquest of these countries by people of the west, only a legacy is left of those civilisations.

Similar civilisations could have emerged in the Cape Colony, Australia and Tasmania if these had not been disrupted by British imperialism, which did not recognise the original inhabitants of these countries as human beings. They were hunted for sport in the Cape colonies and as vermin in Tasmania during the days that these countries became British colonies. Colonialism started during the seventeenth century. By the end of the nineteenth century it had affected the rest of the world. Its motives were to plunder the wealth that could be found in the colonies. In Mexico and Peru the wealth was in mineral form. In Africa it was the slaves, and in India and China it was obtained through trade. The trade was negotiated through concessions and, if this was not possible, it was undertaken by force. The wealth obtained from the colonies led to the desire to occupy some of them so that other nations could not take possession of them. This is shown by the 'scramble for Africa' during the nineteenth century. The wealth from the colonies brought prosperity to Europe, during the Industrial Revolution; it also brought suffering to those families which provided slaves in return for European goods.

The methods used to acquire colonies varied from aggressive invasion to political treaty, with rulers who sought protection but failed to get rid of their protectors. So these became their masters. Then the Europeans settled down, opened up the country by using local labour, and took out of the country more wealth than they had put in. The colonies produced primary products, which were marketed in Europe. If the labour force in the colony was unsuitable, it was brought from other colonies, as was the case with the labour required to construct and operate the East African Railways and the sugar plantations in the West Indies.

There was therefore no real development during the period of the colonial administration. The people of the colonies were educated up to the level where they could be useful to the administrators. Medical facilities were limited to places where the administrators lived. In these places, the workers' welfare was poor and this left problems which were very difficult to solve.

Once political power was handed over by colonists to indigenous people, economic power still remained under the control of the former colonialists, depending upon the markets abroad. This meant that politically independent states were economically controlled from

Europe. The wealth continued to flow from the colonies to Europe and, in a sense, the main objective of colonialism continued to exist. This new type of colonialism goes on with the apparent consent of the independent states. Their political leaders have little choice. Their nations aspire to a higher standard of living. Their material needs are the same as those of people in developed countries. They have to face competition for the goods available, and in any competition one person is bound to win. In economic competition it is those who have most who win.

The problems of Rhodesia, therefore, are as old as the arrival of the British citizens in that country. They originate from the capitals and financial centres of the West, where industrial financial magnates, men who command great respect in their own society, plan to plunder the resources and wealth of the Third World. Citizens of the First World must pay attention to problems in Rhodesia, which arise primarily from the actions and decisions of the British government and citizens. These decisions and actions have adversely affected us ever since the arrival of the white man in Rhodesia.

In 1888 Mr J.S. Moffat, son of the famous missionary and doctor, signed the following British-Matabele Treaty on behalf of the British Crown:

'The Chief Lobengula, ruler of the tribe known as the Amatebele, together with the Mashona and Makaranga tributaries of the same, hereby agrees to the following articles and conditions.

That peace and amity shall continue forever, between Her Britannic Majesty, Her subjects, and the Amatebele people, and the contracting Chief Lobengula engages to use his utmost endeavours to prevent any rupture of the same. To cause the strictest observance of this treaty and to carry

83

out the spirit of the treaty of friendship which was entered into between his late father, the Chief Mzilikazi with the then Governor of the Cape of Good Hope in the year of our Lord 1836.

It is hereby further agreed by Lobengula, Chief in and over the Amatebele country with his tributaries as aforesaid on behalf of himself and his people, that he will refrain from entering into any correspondence or treaty with any foreign state or power to sell, alienate or cede or permit or countenance any sale alienation or session of the whole or any part of the said Amatebele country under his chieftainship, or upon any other subject without the prior knowledge and sanction of Her Majesty's High Commissioner for South Africa.

In faith of which I, Lobengula, on my part have here-onto set my hand at Bulawayo, Matebeleland, this eleventh day of February, and of Her Majesty's reign the fifty-first.'

The Treaty was signed by Lobengula, who put his mark of an X, Mr W. Graham, Mr G.B. van Wyk and Mr J.S. Moffat, the Assistant Commissioner.

Forwarding the British-Matabele Treaty to the Deputy Commissioner, Bechuanaland Protectorate on 11th February 1888, Mr J.S. Moffat wrote as follows:

'I have the honour to forward certified copy of an agreement into which the Chief Lobengula is willing to enter with Her Majesty's Government. He has just put his own hand to it. After protracted discussion and explanation I am thoroughly satisfied that he understands what he has done and that his desires and intentions are fully in accord with the tenor of the document.

There would have been very little hesitation about his signing it, but for the fact that he and his counsellors have been much perplexed by the pretentions which have been put forward by certain visitors to his country to be messengers from the English government more especially by two persons who were here recently and claimed to be on a secret mission to him from Government, with proposals of a much more serious nature than mine.

It was put to me as a serious difficulty, that perhaps in my absence, these or others might come with another kind of message, and how were they to know the true from the false. I referred them to the fact that wide publicity had been given to my mission in so much that every European in the country knew of my coming before I arrived, and also to the fact that I came with an escort of mounted police.

Two Europeans resident in the country were present during the whole discussion, but in view of a bitter feeling which exists here between English and Dutch they preferred that their names should not appear. Those who have signed as witnesses are troopers of the Bechuanaland police. I ought to state, however, that I received the most valuable aid from Mr Tainton who is a skilled linguist and acted when neccessary as interpreter.

I have etc., J.S. Moffat, Assistant Commissioner.'

After the signing of the British-Matabeleland Treaty, Mr C.D. Rudd obtained the rights to all metals and minerals in Lobengula's kingdom on 13 October 1888. Before Lobengula could realise what was happening, the British government granted a Royal Charter on 29 October 1888 to the British South African Company, with the following principal objects:

1 To work the concessions so far as they were valid.
2 To secure other concessions subject to the approval of the Secretary of State.
3 To preserve peace and order.
4 To abolish the slave trade and domestic slavery.
5 To prevent the sale of intoxicant to natives.
6 In the administration of justice, to consider carefully native laws and customs, especially with regard to rights and property.
7 To seek and act upon the advice of the Imperial Authorities.

The question that arises is how could the British South Africa Company administer justice or consider carefully native laws and customs in Lobengula's kingdom or preserve peace and order there, without his permission. The British had sought friendship and minerals, but conquered our people during the 1893 war and the 1896 revolt, and established a colonial administration which was carried out by the British South Africa Company. This was the British people's interpretation of the faith in which Lobengula had signed the British-Matebele Treaty.

They now wish us, Lobengula's descendants, nearly 100 years later, to have the same faith in the Secretary of State and agree to the 1971 proposals for a settlement which I have commented on in the previous c chapter.

Towards the end of colonial rule, in 1918, the Judicial Committee of the Privy Council issued a report which declared that the legal title to land and minerals in Southern Rhodesia was vested in the British Crown. This ruling prevented Southern Rhodesia from choosing to be part of South Africa and allowed it to become a self-governing colony in 1923. In that year, Britain authorized its citizens in Southern Rhodesia to deal with and to decide upon the affairs of the African population who became, and still are, British subjects. The African population was not consulted about this constitutional change. A governor was appointed to represent the Crown in Southern Rhodesia and to consent to, on behalf of the Crown and presumably the British people, all legislation passed by the Parliament of Southern Rhodesia.

During this period the Land Apportionment Act was passed. Its intentions, we are told, were to protect the land interests of the African people, but its outcome was the removal of many African families from their ancestral homes. They were forced off their lands to make place for Europeans who came to settle in Rhodesia at the end of the Second World War. The Act provided for land to be reserved for African use but left the occupation of other land free from any restrictions. Various amendments to the Land Apportionment Act made it possible for the present illegal regime to destroy the homes of the Tangwena people in 1969. The Act is now replaced by the notorious Land Tenure Act which now divides our country into racial and separate areas, giving half of it—45 million acres—to 5½ million Africans, and the other half to 250,000 Europeans. Similar acts of Southern Rhodesian Parliament, like the Native Affairs Act of 1927, and the Native Passes Act of 1939, were passed through the hands of the Queen's Representative in Southern Rhodesia, and have been amended from time to time by the illegal regime to the displeasure of the African population.

The Native Affairs Act, now called the African Affairs Act, requires that 'every African woman who gives birth to a child whose father is European to whom such a woman is not married in terms of the Marriage Act, shall within a period of three months from the date of such birth, give or cause to be given notice thereof to the District Commissioner of the district in which such birth takes place'. Apparently no responsibility is placed upon the father of such a child. The same Act also empowers the Secretary of Internal Affairs to prohibit people from entering or remaining in the Tribal Trust Lands in Rhodesia. The Native Passes Act, now called the African (Registration and Identification) Act requires all Africans to carry certificates of registration, and restricts the movement of Africans from one area to another.

The so-called responsible government, established in 1923, did not make adequate provision for the education of African children. This was left to missionaries who wished to convert our people to Christianity but could not afford to provide secondary education. In 1950 only one government secondary school offered education to Africans up to 'O' level. At present there are 100 secondary schools, of which 83 are run by the churches, and five Sixth Form schools, three of which are also run by the churches. The illegal regime spends an equal sum of money on many African children's education as it does on a few European children's education. This works out at $26 per African child per year, and $285 per European child. The African parent pays school fees while the European child receives free State education. Many European children who failed to qualify to enter the University of Rhodesia have their travel and education expenses to South Africa paid for by the State. African children are compelled by law to start school at the age of seven; European children at the age of five.

African labour was, and is still, being exploited to develop that part of the country now reserved for European use. Little or no provision is made for the development of African areas. Where provision is made, the funds are obtained from extra taxation of the local Africans, or from profits made by Municipalities from sale of African beer. The average annual wages of Africans employed in various jobs is agriculture: $153; mining: $334; manufacturing: $478; electricity and water: $448; building: $428; finance and insurance: $714; restaurants and hotels: $454; transport: $626; public administration: $409; education: $590; health: $579; domestic: $256; and other employment $430.

The average annual wage of Europeans employed in these jobs is more than 10 times the above figures.

Land loss, discriminatory legislation, lack of education and exploitation of labour, continues to happen in a British colony as part of the Western democratic machinery described as responsible government. At first, this British government policy was approved by Parliament at Westminster. Now it is carried out by rebellious British citizens. The British government disregarded this situation in the past; in much the same way it does so at present.

In 1953 the British government established the Federation of Rhodesia and Nyasaland in an attempt to bridge a widening gulf of racial discord. The attempt failed because it was half-hearted, and in reality it sought to establish a horse-and-rider partnership. The white man was to be the rider and the black man the horse. This led to the wrath and frustration of African people, who expressed it through the African National Movement in Southern Rhodesia which became firmly established as from 1957. During the federation the African's desire to end their second-class citizenship in the country of their birth grew. The African showed that they understood democracy, but failed to understand that their oppression was caused by an intentional policy of the Rhodesian government, encouraged by the British government. Any desire to improve the position of the African population was dangerous for any Rhodesian leader, as Mr Garfield Todd discovered in 1957. The Whitehead Administration, between 1958 and 1962, resorted to banning the nationalist movement and to detaining its leaders without trial. It introduced the Emergency Powers Act, the Law and Order Maintenance Act, and the Unlawful Organisations Act which removed power from the courts, and gave unlimited power to the Security Police and Government Ministers.

In 1961 Mr Duncan Sandys, who was the Secretary of State for the Commonwealth Office, introduced a new constitution for Southern Rhodesia. The Constitution was rejected by African leaders during the negotiation stages, on the grounds that it offered too little, too late.

After the dissolution of the Federation of Rhodesia and Nyasaland in 1963, the right wing of the Rhodesia Front Party, which had won the elections in 1962, took control of that Party in 1964. Mr Ian Smith replaced Mr Winston Field as Prime Minister and declared UDI in 1965. This was a treacherous act, which the British Government have in fact condoned by making proposals seeking to grant lawful independence to the gang of traitors. This is shown by the Smith-Home 1971 proposals for a settlement. This action of the British Government led many of us to realise that HMG interests are unquestionably the same as those of the traitors.

We can now understand, and see in their perspective the British Government's actions in 1888, 1923, and 1961 which would have been different if its interests were not those of the colonialists.

Following Mr Smith's UDI in 1965, Mr Wilson, the British Prime Minister, declared that Her Majesty's Government would not use force to bring down the illegal regime. There was much talk of the kith and kin ties between Britain and Rhodesia, and obviously Mr Wilson's red herring won the day. It would have been better if he had not made this declaration, particularly after he had travelled all the way to Rhodesia to confer with Mr Smith.

The attitude of the present British Government is that it is 'unwilling to use force because of the danger that it would create a racial conflagration in Southern Africa which would be in the interests neither of the Europeans nor the Africans'. The British Government is conveniently ignoring that it is itself a white government and that the kith and kin argument applies both ways. Besides that, if Britain used force, her NATO allies might presumably support her actions. This would leave South Africa alone to defend the illegal regime, but unfortunately, in accordance with the British government's 'legal obligations under the Simonstown Agreement for the defence of the Cape sea routes, Britain supplies maritime defence equipment to South Africa'. Because of this the South African regime can concentrate its military resources on its internal security which includes the defence of the illegal regime in Rhodesia; it also makes it possible for South Africa to continue its policy of apartheid. In any case, there is no reason why the British Government should be bound up by the Simonstown Agreement which the South African regime is not honouring.

Britain is being compelled by the United Nations to observe and intensify sanctions against Rhodesia. It refuses to have them intensified, previously on the grounds that Africans would be badly affected but, when this deliberately false logic was pointed out to them, the British Government now says:

'The reason for which we have opposed the intro-
duction of new sanction measures, is not their effect
on the African people of Rhodesia, but our belief
that it is pointless to consider further measures until
the existing sanctions are applied effectively and

conscientiously by the international community.'
The British Government would be more honest if it
said that the reason is that severe sanctions would bring
down the illegal regime, instead of placing the blame on
the international community.

The British Government's contention that the rights
of the indigenous people of Rhodesia would have been
restored if we had accepted the 1971 proposals for a
settlement is a false one. Apart from granting legal
independence to the illegal regime, the proposals seek
to leave the political and economic power in the hands
of the rebels and even to entrench it. The proposals
state that: 'the Constitution will be the constitution
adopted in Rhodesia in 1969. The Rhodesian government have intimated to the British Government their
firm intention within the spirit of these proposals to
make progress towards ending racial discrimination.'
A careful study of the franchise qualifications outlined
in the proposals about the employment and income
statistics shows that it will take centuries before many
Africans are qualified to vote. It is a shame that the
British Government should be conniving with traitors
in this way. We rejected these proposals simply because
they are not honorable but, as if this was not enough,
the British Government now requires us to negotiate
for our rights with rebellious thieves.

In keeping its offer of a settlement on the table
despite the fact that it was rejected by the people of
Rhodesia as a whole, Britian is adopting an ignominious
silence, concerning the 5½ million Africans for whom
it is the trustee. There is no whisper of protest from
the British Government about those who are being detained or murdered by the regime. More gravely, the
British Government is keeping the offer on the table

while Mr Smith is making a series of repressive measures against the Africans, such as the Pass Laws, the removal of Africans from the north of the country, the Bill setting up Provincial Authorities, the exclusion of missionaries from African areas and the imposition of collective fines.

The British Foreign Secretary does not say that these actions are a betrayal of the proposals. His silence seems to imply that the Africans had it coming to them when they rejected the proposals for a settlement. Mr Smith, on the other hand, says that none of the measures that he is imposing affect the settlement. They are necessary in the national interests. The 1971 proposals themselves allow him to act in that way where national interests over-ride other considerations. So, if the Africans had accepted the proposals, Mr Smith would now be acting as if he had the consent of the Africans. If a settlement were imposed by governments rather than agreed to by people of Rhodesia as a whole, it should be emphasised that no African worth the name would value any kind of a settlement which grants legal independence to unfaithful traitors.

After the Pearce Report there can be no doubt about our people's reasoning. We want equal rights in our country. It is not something that we should ask for cap in hand, but what every human being is entitled to.

The British imperial power first imposed itself upon African people in Rhodesia by deception, as we have seen. The Smith regime in Rhodesia began by an act of blatant illegality, and it has been sustained ever since by the use of illegal political force against the black people in Rhodesia. This is why the liberation movement is fighting, and where the struggle begins.

The Liberation Movement of Southern Africa is

made up of young men who have staked their lives for the sake of others. I have shared cells with some of them at Salisbury Remand Prison. Even after many years of imprisonment most of them are as determined as ever. They operate within Frelimo, ZAPU, ZANU, Frolizi, the African National Congress of South Africa, and SWAPO. They are based in Zambia, Tanzania, Mozambique and Caprivi Strip, and are the responsibility of the OAU's Liberation Committee, headed by Major-General Ashim Mbita of Tanzania.

Some members of the African Nationalist Movement long ago began to prepare for the liberation of our country from outside its borders. They left the country or were recruited abroad to train as guerilla fighters and gain support from the countries which help them. These included Communist countries. These members of the African Nationalist Movement are the freedom fighters who enter the country from across the Zambesi. All people extol their patriotic young men when they fight for their country and the churches bless their flags and pray for the peaceful rest of those who die in battle. They are not duped terrorists but heroes. Our freedom fighters are acting against a government which usurped power illegally and which they and the majority of our people within the country and most countries through the world regard as illegal. The freedom fighters' policy is not 'to use methods inspiring extreme fear in order to coerce'. It is rather, as the security department in Rhodesia must know very well, to avoid engagement with the security forces, infiltrate into the country and co-operate with the local people. They may inspire fear in some just as the rebel regime inspires fear in many throughout the world. This however, does not justify the use of the term 'terrorists' for those of our people who are engaged in the liberation of our country.

Many people in the world today consider that the time has come for mankind to follow seriously the more excellent way of love. So there are many who cannot, on principle, applaud the violence used by the Rhodesia Front regime or, in times of defence by the freedom fighters. But we are living in a world where force is widely used and approved by many, including the Christian churches. It is generally regarded as more justified when a people uses it to defend their integrity, rather than to destory that of others. We regard the force used by the rebel regime as a great evil and that used by the freedom fighters as defence of their rights. In any case, it has always been regarded a valid Christian service to succour those who find themselves involved in the use of force.

Whether or not our people should defend their rights violently is a matter of individual opinion. Violence is defined as the unlawful exercise of physical force. Is 'the transgression, infringement action against the dictates of the requirements of law' justifiable to bring about change in Rhodesia? The answer lies in the fact that there has been no law in Rhodesia, since the illegal declaration of independence. The freedom fighters connot be unlawfully exercising physical force because there is no lawful Authority to judge what is lawful or unlawful in Rhodesia. As the illegal regime is unlawful, those seeking to remove it cannot be acting unlawfully. The illegal declaration of independence was by a tiny minority of the Rhodesian population, 55,000. It was the cynical breaking of the law which matters to the world.

A time will come when men will not fear guns, interrogation cells, police informers, or the Gonakudzingwa detention camp; they will cross the Zambesi to return home greater men, determined, disciplined and equipped to penetrate into their country not as terrorists but as liberators. They may suffer, die, linger in the Salisbury Remand Prison in Class D cells or be hunted through the country together with those who harbour them. But many will endure, and they will ultimately achieve their goal.

The Liberation Movement has been operating in Rhodesia for a long time. Their incursion into the country was reported on 21 December 1972. From the press we learned that many people were killed, that Mr Gerald Hawkesworth was captured (and was subsequently released in December 1973); two of his companions were killed. Mr Leslie Jellicoe who was on holiday in Rhodesia also lost his life. All this and the death of many of our people fighting in the Zambesi Valley could have been prevented if the right action had been taken at the right time. However, fear of the liberation movement prompted Mr Smith to visit Portugal suddenly in 1972 and to talk with Mr Botha, the South African defence Minister.

Smith must be living through a period of continuous nightmare now that the Zambian Government has suspended its foreign exchange dealings with Rhodesia, and is rerouting its copper after Mr Smith's decision to blockade the Zambian border. He is afraid of the Liberation Movement operating on two fronts, Zambia and Mozambique. Mr Jack Howman of the Rhodesia Defence believes that Botswana is also being used as the third front, Mr Smith realises that the whites in Rhodesia are out-numbered 21−1. The excellent Rhodesian forces are too small to contain a significant Guerilla pressure from two fronts. Smith can no longer

rely on the African chiefs. He may soon find it danger-
our to recruit Africans in the armed service. Lengthen-
ing the conscription period may save him for a time, but
the call up of reservists means that the skilled labour
necessary for the weakening economy would be used
for defence instead of strengthening that economy.

How South Africa and Portugal can become involved
in the defence of Rhodesia depends on the British
Government. It can stop Portugal's interference through
NATO, and South Africa's interference by prohibiting
the sale of arms to South Africa. This would leave the
Rhodesian whites alone on the defensive. Divided, they
would find it difficult to face the better trained guerillas.
The latter are still few, but their number will grow as
fast as their success, once the African people realise
that they are destined to win. The victory could come
sooner if sanctions weakened the Rhodesian economy
to a point where its superior organisation and tech-
nology could be challenged. A community of 250,000
whites cannot face a population of 5½ million poten-
tial enemies. This will bring Smith to his knees. All
Southern Africa could be involved in a conventional
war sooner than we think. Urgent steps could be taken
to prevent a Vietnam-type situation, by creating harmony between black and white. This is the real crux
of the future security of the white man and will involve
the removal of all obnoxious race measures and the
creation of a machinery for regular consultation and
cooperation between all races without delay.

Is what is happening the beginning of the end of
white domination in Rhodesia? With Smith's intel-
ligence machine looking embarrassingly incompetent,
he is now attempting to launch a new sanction-busting
campaign. He has draught and the guerilla threats to

deal with. His ill-judged manoeuvres are a source of our strength.

I do not believe that there would ever be a more right wing regime than Mr Smith's to bid for power. If he seeks more military support from South Africa it will not change the course of events at the present moment, but only make the situation worse. This may cause the whites to come to a conference table with the African National Council, and I hope that the ANC will press for nothing less than majority rule. If this does not please Mr Smith, he will approach the British Government, who must now be anxious to get rid of the Rhodesian problem. The British Government could hand the problem over to the United Nations, or it might acquiesce in the creation of black homelands; neither will end the present troubles.

The present rebellion of the colonist government is more than a technicality; it is a continuous crime of violence and treason. The British Government has not used a police force against its errant citizens but agreed with the United Nations to impose sanctions which are subverted by business men.

The odium which attaches to the British Government derives from its unwillingness to get rid of the illegal regime that has usurped power. There are many weapons in Britain's armoury: consititutional, diplomatic, political, economic, and, as Mr Wilson pointed out in 1965, in certain circumstances, military. The breakdown of law, and in many instances, order, in the colony should be restored by the British Government which is the legal government of the colony. It should fulful its responsibilities which are constitutional, historical and moral.

In his book 'Violence', Jacques Ellul says that

'According to theologians, seven conditions must co-
incide to make a war just: 1) the cause fought for must
itself be just; 2) the purpose of the warring power
must remain just while hostilities go on; 3) the war
must truly be the last resort, all peaceful means having
been exhausted; 4) the methods employed during the
war to vanquish the foe must themselves be just; 5) the
benefits the war can reasonably be expected to bring
for mankind must be greater than the evils provoked
by the war itself; 6) victory must be ensured, and
7) the peace concluded at the end of the war must be
just and of such a nature as to prevent new war.'

The cause to liberate the people of Rhodesia is a
just one: it will remain just while hostilities go on. Our
people's human rights are greater than the evil provoked by apartheid imposed on us by foreigners. In
guerilla warfare the guerillas never lose. Peace comes
only after war which will be just in Rhodesia, where
our people's desire for peace has put off for so long
the decision to fight. In the struggle for our liberation
and for justice, which may take many shapes, our
people must never forget that they are struggling
against British imperialism in all its forms. Our struggle
for human dignity in our own country can, and must
be, seen by the rest of the world population as a
struggle for human degnity in the world at large. This
alone is a good cause for the struggle.

7

Black and White

Strictly speaking there are no white or black people but people of shades between pink and brown. Nonetheless, black and white in the southern African context denote oppression, class and privilege. In Rhodesia the oppressed are black and the privileged white. But do not get the idea that the oppressed will no longer seek their liberation when the colour of their oppressors change.

How deep is the alienation of black and white people? How much good is there still in their societies? In the African society this good is seen in their moral strength, nourished by what remains of tribal religion and custom: the close link with our ancestors; the living family; the extended family; the way of life evolved over many centuries. Recently, this has of course been modified by Christianity through the narrow outlook of some missionaries. Christianity threatens, and sometimes uproots our traditional way of life. The influence of the new religion brought with it our conquest, and we are at present identifying the behaviour of the missionaries with that of their countrymen who rule us illegally with the blessing of some churchmen in Rhodesia.

No civilisation, and therefore no people, can claim to be Christian if the aim is to suppress for ever one section of the community and to deny it all the economic benefits that are striven for. The wide difference of feeling between the 'haves' and 'have nots' is deepened by the difference in race between the two halves of the same community, and a feeling that it is wrong for the 'haves' to misuse power by forcing rotten policies down the throats of the 'have nots'.

Let us imagine how the pattern of life of Rhodesian blacks has changed because the political scandal of the whites has forced African political leaders either to escape from the country to live in exile or to remain there under detention. The vacuum caused by their absence causes increasing racial and social segregation. Forced movements of the African communities; lack of educational opportunities, particularly in the higher and technical fields; lack of employment has, generally speaking, made classes out of people's colours. Let us at the same time bear in mind these two articles of the Universal Declaration of Human Rights by the General Assembly of the United Nations:

1 'All human beings are born free and equal in dignity and rights. They are endowed with reason and conscience and should act towards one another in a spirit of brotherhood.'
2 'Everyone is entitled to all the rights and freedoms set forth in this Declaration without distinction of any kind, such as race, colour, sex, language, religion, political or other opinion, national or social origin, property, birth, or other status. Furthermore, no distinction shall be made on the basis of the political, jurisdictional or international status of the country or territory to which the person belongs, whether it be Independent, Trust, Non Self-governing or under any other limitation of Sovereignty.'

Oppression involves two parties: the oppressor and

the oppressed. It is the oppressed who must struggle for fuller humanity. But the oppressor cannot recognize the wickedness of his actions, and where he does, he tries to justify them by more wicked actions. The oppressor dislikes progress and organic growth. He likes to possess, and when he loses control of possessions, his world comes to an end. He regards other human beings as lifeless possessions which will benefit and fulfil his own world. His civilization is one where everything must be like himself, and in this process he 'eats' people. He destroys the other human beings' personalities, and leaves them out of harmony with themselves, with those in their society and in their world. This is what makes a shame of the Rhodesian white man's civilization in the black man's mind.

His civilization is one where the black man must be humiliated every day, by being referred to in derogatory terms like Kaffir, Native, Bantu, Boy, or Girl, regardless of age. The black man must be discriminated against socially and laws are made to enforce it. The white man does this with laws that are intended to safeguard the interests of the black man, in the hope that the black man will not realise that 'Eurpeans only' means that the blackman's interests are excluded. These interests may be as simple as passing urine, feeding a hungry stomach, or finding a roof to put one's head under. And when the black man asks the simple question, 'What civilization is this that does not allow him to pass urine in a modern city in the middle of his country?' he becomes an agitator to be locked up in prison, all his life, because he might ask this question too often in the audience of other black men. The white man's civilization will end when too many blacks want to urinate in the same place as the white man.

Yet the whites in Rhodesia say that their brand of civilization is Christian, which must keep the Africans silent. Our silence is one of fear, of disappointment. It is a dangerous one for the Christian world. In our silence we consider what Christianity is. Is it the preservation of privilege for the few 'haves', and the humiliation of the many 'have nots'? Have we been deceived by the missionaries who taught us the white man's religion in exchange for our land, our dignity and our humanity? Shall we accept to remain the white man's hewer of wood and drawers of water, and leave them to control us so ignorantly? The answer is 'No'! And this was expressed fearlessly to the Pearce Commission.

The Christian world must face the fact that a large part of the world population is non-Christian, even in countries that claim a Christian civilization. Christians all over the world teach their followers about the evils of communism, but fail to see the evil which is going on in their midst. They spend time repeating what the Bible teaches: 'Take the beam that is in your eye out, so that you can see to remove the mote in your brother's eye.' Does this mean 'fill your stomach first in order to be strong enough to exploit your bretheren'?

The oppressed black, like other oppressed people the world over, is regarded as if he came into existence eighty years ago. He may only have been known by the white then, but those who believe in evolution must have told the whites that the process takes more than just eighty years.

In our villages of an earlier day, even now our families have communal responsibility and respect which provided our grandfathers with their only source of security. Were they and those who lived before our grandfathers better off than most of us today? The life in villages is simple, but the pattern is well set out. Relationships are laid down, and everyone fits well into them. Success in life means achieving a collective harmony; it is asking for no more than the rest have. Those who go out to hunt buck or other animals for food, share it out in the community, according to well-known and defined convention. The hunter gets his portion, and so does the mother-in-law, and the elderly woman who lives next door. We are told that this is primitive, that our way of life is 'pagan'.

Those of us who believed these assertions, have gone out to the towns in search of white man's civilization, to Salisbury and Bulawayo. What do we find but loneliness and a deep sense of insecurity, with no roof over your head, among anonymous people, each tries to grab for himself the most that he can. Even those who do not drink beer may go to the beer-hall to escape from their single room, often shared with friends. But it is in the beer halls that the police informers operate. The politically conscious try to avoid them, which may mean loss of contact with those they want to influence.

In this one-roomed life in our African townships, security of tenure depends on the landlords ability to keep his tenancy going, because the landlord is in turn renting the house from the Department of African Housing controlled by the regime. This, and the eyes of the Security Police, is the cause of fear that silences us black people in the urban areas. This deep sense of insecurity is finding its way to the tribal areas, through the Land Tenure Act.

Gradually the black man becomes one with those whom he feels are the brave ones, but whose ranks he does not join until the Security Police drags him out for questioning at the Central Police Station. Then he moves into a world where men think of suffering as an inescapable service to their fellow men, where they have peace of mind. Perhaps here some Christians will start to learn to live in 'here and now' rather than in the next life.

Ever since the Rhodesian Front took power in 1962, it has emphasized racial segregation and differences. This European society, aware that its privileged economic and social position depends on retaining power in the hands of the whites, puts an unbearable yoke on the Africans. Every so often the yoke becomes too heavy and resentment takes its place. This is a tragedy in human relationships.

Because black people know that it is more important to be human than white, we have got to fight for the restoration of our humanity as individuals. We suffer the effects of oppression more than our oppressors, so we understand the necessity for liberation and recognise the need to fight for it. Therefore we shall be performing an act of love which opposes the lack of love which lies at the heart of Rhodesian Front policies, and some of the Church Leaders' false generosity. We are discovering that the white man's oppression continues because we tolerate it, and sometimes nurse it. Like every weed, it grows faster than the wanted plant. It is up to us to pluck out these weeds before they have grown too big. If our grandfathers had not acted as hosts to the white men in 1888 we, their grandchildren, would not be in our present situation. But God the Father and God the Son, who knows all things, surely knows that we want freedom. He will not bring it to us on a silver plate.

There are many risks involved in taking our freedom, but they are worthwile risks, and better than living in one room in a township, a tribal trust land, a prison cell, or in exile in the oppressors' land. Without freedom we cannot exist as a people but as oppressed individual objects, to be manipulated by the oppressors. Freedom means that we should be responsible, and not tolerate any kind of oppression. Our humanity was destroyed through conquest and we must struggle as men rather than objects to regain our humanity. The strife will be over when battles are won.

There are many battles to be won, not least that against some Church leaders in Rhodesia who boast of 'the wonderful work they do in Rhodesia, confirming thousands of Christians every year', and fail to realize that they live in two worlds: one for the people they confirm, and the other, for themselves. When they come home they talk of the atrocities of Africa, the ignorance and disease. Let them not forget that there is a bigger percentage of non-Christians in Britain; these Church leaders never dream of establishing missions to convert their own people. The Bible is full of references to private property and teachings about attitudes to property. Christian missions in Rhodesia have wanted land, money to build schools, hospitals, churches and farms. The minute these things become more important than one's neighbour, they must be got rid of. Do some churches not lay treasure in Rhodesia where thieves steal black people's land, side by side with starving and unclothed people? And recently how many Christian chaplains have been sent to the illegal army and prisons? Have any been sent to pray for the Freedom fighters? Perhaps this is as it should be because at present most Church leaders are white.

Church leaders issued a statement about the Land

Tenure Act, which said, 'We totally disagree with the continuance of the underlying principle of dividing Rhodesia into two distinct racial areas, neither of which can be occupied by members of the other race, except by specific permission of a minister of Government . . .'. But a study of church organisation and the way of living on many a mission land reveals nothing different from the sort of living they condemn.

The Christian form of worship is totally alien to the majority of Christians in Africa. Many of the people who are confirmed still believe in worship through our ancestors; many of the African clergy still seek healing through Nganga. Maybe priesthood is just a profession, like being a teacher, both require salaries and long training.

Up till recent times the Church has provided schooling. Now that the Church no longer does this, there may be less and less people going to confirmation or even to Church. Our people supported the Church because it provided education. Through learning to read and write, we became aware of ourselves, and began to look critically at the world around us and the situation in which we find ourselves. Those who are educated are often asked to take the initiative to act, to transform our society, which gives them the opportunity to participate. In this sense, education has been a subversive force, and the missionaries must be thanked for providing it. But having done so, they should not now condemn their efforts and those of their predecessors, in order to appease the illegal regime.

The world is not standing still. It looks to many that our vocation as people is to transform our world and move towards a fuller community life. In this task our personal dignity and natural 'belonging together', which

107

alone can save the world from becoming a jungle, must be emphasized. We in Rhodesia call ourselves 'wanhu', 'Abantu', the people. People are individuals who have a tradition, something worked out, by good relationships before the white man came. Destroying us as people destroys our tradition, and vice versa.

Part of this tradition is that we have had kings, who are now referred to as 'chiefs'. They were concerned with maintaining the dispensing law. The present chiefs must have split personalities to uphold immoral laws, the main purpose of which is to maintain white supremacy. True chiefs, like Munhuwepasi Mangwende and Rekayi Tangwena upheld their traditional roles of chieftainship, and found themselves unwanted by the white governments. Munhuwepasi Mangwende was deposed, and Rekayi Tangwena is being chased up and down the hills of his land.

Many white Rhodesians fail to accept the fact that they share Rhodesia with a black majority. They constantly goad and prod us as if they are afraid of us, even when we are friendly, disciplined and patient. Those of us who keep dogs on a chain, may deceive ourselves by thinking that the dog likes it. But even the best tempered animal gets sick of ill-willed pestering. We may show this aggressiveness against our own people, if they behave like the white man. If we defend our personality vis à vis our brothers, then we can defend it better against the white man.

Will indiscriminate bloodshed and violence make an impression on the whites? Our present leaders seem to realize that it will do neither the whites, nor ourselves, much good. But if the moment does come it will be simply the result of unendurable provocation; of treading too long on a patience that has its limits. The patience will continue as at present. When the limit is reached nobody will give the signal for violence, there will be no need to.

8
Why Bother?

'I sit on a Man's Back choking him and making him carry me and yet I assure myself and others that I'm sorry for him and wish to lighten his load by all possible means except by getting off his back.' So wrote Tolstoy. Should we bother about this? Why bother that those nations of the world that claim to have benefited most from democracy commit the worst offences against us?

Father Adrian Hastings exposed the atrocities committed by the Portuguese government in Mozambique. It is common knowledge that the NATO's aid to Portugal makes this possible. Portugal could not hold its position in the wars going on in Angola and Mozambique without such help. Those who have been in Portugal inform us that it is one of the poorest countries in Europe. So poor in fact, they say, that it is hardly able to manufacture toys for Portuguese children to play with. Should it not bother us that the same poor nation is able to use great jet bombers and sophisticated weapons to suppress the people of Angola and Mozambique?

Should it not bother us that Christian nations in the West refused to help Tanzania to construct the railway line between Dar-es-Salaam and Lusaka, on the grounds that it was uneconomic, and that the Chinese have agreed to finance it as well as to supply man-power to get on with the job? The Bible says 'and whosoever should compel thee to go a mile go with him twain'. Are the Chinese in fact acting better than Christians? In the struggle between the 'haves' and the 'have nots', are the non-Christian nations not acting better than those that bring up Christ whenever it suits them?

Apartheid in South Africa has been condemned by all people, including the South Africans themselves. Black South Africa suffers from its oppression and exploitation. There is an alternative form of government which the South African minority are refusing to follow. Should we be bothered that the British Government supports this regime with arms and disregards the United Nation's proposals about Namibia?

Apart from being an insult to the black people of Rhodesia, the Rhodesian Front government rebelled against the British crown. Yet the British Minister of State referred to those who are trying to remove the rebels as terrorists.

Should we not bother that most of the white population in Rhodesia are British citizens holding British passports and would be protected by the British Government if the situation in Rhodesia got worse? If the British Government had made it difficult for rebels to renew their passports, it could have become an important non-violent weapon. Instead the British Government does all that it can to facilitate the renewal of passports through Pretoria. The result is that most White Rhodesians have British passports and Black Rhodesians have the illegal Rhodesia Passports. The effect of non-recognition of the Rhodesia passports therefore weighs heavily against the Rhodesian blacks and has no effect on the Rhodesian whites whom it is intended to influence. The few black Rhodesians who hold British passports have to have them renewed at the end of every six months.

Every time that the question of sanctions has been raised the British Government pretends to worry most about their effect on the African population. Time and again we have pointed out that the black people in Rhodesia have nothing to lose through sanctions. Unemployment in the country has existed for years before the rebellion, and will not be made worse by sanctions. The little effect that sanctions have on the white population is what the British Government really worries about. The great sanction hole that exists at Lourenço Marques, where most of the oil comes through into Rhodesia, has been pointed out to Her Majesty's Government many times but disregarded.

Since 1964 African leaders have lingered in prisons and under detention. Some of them, like Maurice Nyagumbo and Daniel Madzimbamuto have suffered fourteen years of detention. From a court proceeding held in 1969, it is quite plain that Daniel Madzimbamuto should now be a free man. Section 1 of the British Government Southern Rhodesia Act states: 'it is hereby declared that Southern Rhodesia continues to be part of Her Majesty's dominion, and that the government and parliament of the United Kingdom have responsibility and jurisdiction as heretofore for and in respect of Southern Rhodesia.' The responsibility has been clearly exercised in the release of Mr Peter Nieswand. Could the same not be applied to many African people held under conditions much worse than he was subjected to.

Why should we bother that the present British Government is keeping on the table the 1971 proposals for a settlement which were rejected by the people of

Rhodesia as a whole? Most of the members of the executive of the African National Council in Rhodesia which was instrumental in rejecting these proposals have been detained.

The proposals themselves are a result of an agreement between the illegal regime and Her Majesty's Government. At the time of writing, the Head of the Rhodesian desk, the Minister of State for Foreign and Commonwealth Affairs, the Foreign Secretary and Mr Smith have Scottish blood in them. Her Majesty's Government considers that agreement should be established between black and white people in Rhodesia before any new move can be made, and the proposals must form a basis of that new move. During any discussions which may take place between the African National Council and the illegal regime in Rhodesia, it is up to ANC to convince both the illegal regime and HMG. On the two occasions that I was a member of groups that went to see the Minister of State for Foreign and Commonwealth Affairs, I was left in no doubt that I would have heard exactly the same points of view if the groups had been talking with Mr Ian Smith.

Why should we bother that our people were conquered violently in 1893 by British citizens who disrupted our culture and civilization, which can be traced back to great kingdoms such as those of King Munomutapa? Why should we bother in fact that deceptive treaties were devised by British people between the English people and our King Lobengula? That in 1918 the Judicial Committee of the Privy Council ruled that the minerals and land in Southern Rhodesia belonged to the British Crown? That when it suits a minority regime, it can break its own laws and can impose on other people the most derogatory laws? That in their own country the Tangwena people are at present living in the mountains and have lost all their property? That in the country of our own birth we are in fact not equal with other people before the law and are compelled to carry pieces of paper to identify ourselves? That the limit of the franchise is so high that it is beyond the means of most Africans? That during the last eleven years the administration of Rhodesia has fallen in the hands of a fascist regime, very similar to that which existed under Nazi Germany?

Most of Europe took a decisive step during the Second World War to end fascism of Italy. Germany and Japan. African forces were enrolled and took part in that war. Similar elements of fascism now exist in Angola, Mozambique, Rhodesia and South Africa; and Britain, who talked of fighting to its last man during the Second World War, is the nation with the biggest financial interest in these countries. In other words, fascism was an evil when it was against the British interests but a blessing when it is in favour of those interests.

Indeed Christianity played a great part when treaties with our Kings were made. After our people were conquered by the white man, missionaries were given vast amounts of land and a free hand in African affairs. But now the same missionaries require a special permit before they can go to say Mass to a dying African in the Tribal Trust Land.

Until 1940 African children were given presents to get them to go to school. Admittedly this was done by missionaries but the point is that, now that the Africans have seen the benefit and importance of education, the regime puts the most severe financial restriction on

African education. You will rightly say that education requires great expenditure of money on the part of the Government. Yes it does, and many good governments are proud to make such an expenditure for the benefit of their people and countries. The question is why it should be too expensive for the government of Rhodesia to provide education for all Africans in Rhodesia but not too expensive for the governments of Zambia or Malawi to do the same. The point I am hoping to make is that Africans in Malawi and Zambia have benefited more since Independence ten years ago. They have made great strides ahead of Rhodesia in the welfare of black people. In the field of education these nations would be where they were eleven years ago if they had not become independent. The British Government would still be telling their people what a wonderful idea the Federation of Rhodesia and Nyasaland was just as they are telling us how wonderful the 1971 proposals for a settlement were.

Franz Fanon in *The Wretched of the Earth* puts forward the same point of view as Germain Greer in *The Female Eunuch*—that what makes us bother is our conscience. We have a body and soul and the ability to love and hate. We know when our body is being misused and when our soul is being tormented. We know when we are being loved or hated. As people we are capable of making judgements and acting in accordance with them. When a man judges that the hate and misery that he has to endure is not really the result of ignorance, but a calculated design to keep those people down, one cannot help but to seek change and the change must be quick, revolutionary. Germain Greer advocates a peaceful revolution and Franz Fanon a violent one.

The Africans in Rhodesia were told that they must have a democratic organisation before they could be given power and so the African National Congress came into being in 1957. In *The African Predicament in Rhodesia*, G.C. Grant summarizes the policy of the ANC as follows; 'The African National Congress of Southern Rhodesia is a People's Movement . . . . Its aim is National Unity of all inhabitants of the country, in true partnership regardless of race, colour and creed. It stands for a completely integrated society, equality of opportunity in every sphere and the social, economic, and political advancement of all . . . Congress is not a racial movement. It is equally opposed to tribalism. It welcomes as members all of any race . . . . It recognizes the rights of all who are citizens of the country whether African, European, Coloured or Asian, to retain permanently the fullest citizenship. It believes that this country can only advance through non-racial thinking and acting, and that an integrated society provides the only alternative to tribalism and racialism. Congress believes that in all of Southern and Eastern Africa there are three outstanding needs which it is supremely important to meet:

(a) The standard of living of millions of people must be raised in a short space of time, through their rapid social, economic and political advancement.

(b) This is only possible with the aid of skills, techniques and capital from overseas. These must be attracted to this country, not only by the offer of material advantages but also by appeal to the altruism and sense of service prevalent in the world.

This is a challenge to the more advanced and privileged people in the world whose help is required in the interest of world peace and total development of Mankind

Congress realizes that to meet these three needs is a task of gigantic proportion, but believes that nothing short of this can ensure the peaceful development of this country for the benefit of all its inhabitants. Congress is therefore dedicated to the fulfilment of the needs, and regards it as a matter of the most urgent necessity...'

This party, the African National Congress, was banned in February 1959. The National Democratic Party (NDP) was formed in January 1960, and banned in December 1961. At that time ZAPU was formed, and it was banned in September 1962. So it does not surprise us that the emergence of ZANU, brought with it a new strategy of violent revolution, which will largely influence developments in Rhodesia.

The talks that are going on between the leaders of the Rhodesia Front and Bishop Muzurewa's African National Council are due to ZANU incursions in the north-east of Rhodesia, as well as the effects of the United Nations sanctions against Rhodesia. Those people sitting on our backs will find it a dangerous place to continue to sit, although they will use every kind of distorted reason to remain there. They will say that the nationalists are not the true representatives of the people. They will point to the chiefs as the traditional representatives of the Africans. This may sound convincing at first sight, but chiefs are now appointed by the Secretary of Internal Affairs, in terms of the African Affairs Act. Why should the Secretary of Internal Affairs play this role in the appointment of traditional chiefs? Chief Tangwena is one of the traditional chiefs, recognised as such by the African people in Rhodesia and appointed in the traditional way, but look at what the regime is doing to him and to his people.

Those who ride on the backs of other human beings
will shout about tribalism, when an African from
Mashonaland disagrees with one from Matabeleland.
No one justifies any form of tribalism, but it is specially
unjustifiable to think that it is tribalism which makes
people disagree. We are each one of us born in some
tribal group. We do not suddenly discard this when we
become leaders, neither do we lose our capacity to
disagree when we are in positions of leadership. It is
amazing that when Mr Smith disagrees with Mr Wilson
no one attributes this to tribalism, even though it is a
well known fact that there are strong Scottish, Welsh,
English and Irish feelings.

Many people in our country recognize the historical
fact of the existence of tribes, but tribalism recently
has had less and less influence. There are many tribes
in Rhodesia: Ndau, Bunji, Manyika, Maungwe, Karanga,
Nyanja, Ndebele, Zezuru, Korekore, to mention a few.
The people who see tribalism among the black people
in Rhodesia, talk about it in terms of the Shona tribe
versus the Ndebele. They never talk of tribalism when
a Shona person does not get on well with a Nyanja
person. In Rhodesia, as wlsewhere in the world, there
are a substantial number of marriages between people
of different tribes. Great friendships exist between
Nyanja, Shona and Ndebele people. There are disagree-
ments as well. Divorces occur all over the world and in
some families children and their parents fail to get
along with one another. Can all this be attributed to
tribalism? Surely where there are two or more possible
courses of action people's opinions can differ. Why
must black people's opinions be always the same? Why
are they referred to as tribal only when they differ?

The man who sits on another man's back knows that he is taking a risk. He will claim that his human horse is mad when he makes it gallop towards a dangerous situation for him. He will tag at the reins and get annoyed with the 'horse' for wanting to get rid of him or to take a similar risk. He will assure himself and others that he is doing this for the benefit of the 'horse' rather than himself.

Think of another analogy: that of a parasite—a tick —and its host—a cow. The parasite exists only as long as the host does. Every good farmer knows the importance of keeping his cows free of ticks. He puts them through a spray of arsenic. If he fails to do this, he exposes his cows to every kind of tick-borne disease and so provides a good food supply for the vultures. The cows may die off only one by one but in the end they will all perish.

In the Rhodesian situation there are many honourable human riders. The good farmers linger in prisons. Our people are herded all over the country like cows. They either run the risk of going through a spray of arsenic—revolution—and emerge rid of some of their 'ticks' or they continue to carry their parasites and march fearlessly towards the vultures which devour our wealth and dignity. It is true that in a revolution many lives may be lost but they will not all perish.

This is why we bother. The Rhodesian situation raises important issues of conscience. Until recently we had the patience to wait, and the hope that the situation will be changed by those who imposed it. We have now gathered strength to change the situation because it ought to be changed. And indeed, I believe, we have the wisdom to do so.

9

God and Caesar

'And they sent out unto him their disciples with the
Herodians, saying "Master we know that thou art
true and teachest the way of God in truth. Neither
carest thou for any man, for thou regardest not the
person of man. Tell us therefore what thinkest thou.
Is it lawful to give tribute unto Caesar?' But Jesus
perceived their wickedness and said "Why tempt ye
me, ye hypocrites. Show me the tribute money."
And they brought unto him a penny. And he said
unto them "Whose is this image and superscription?"
They said unto him "Caesar's." Then said he unto
them "Render therefore unto Caesar the things
which are Caesar's and unto God the things that
are God's." '

The distinction between God and Caesar is quite
clear. The one is above the other, both should be
acceptable. The biblical Caesar was legitimate. It was
proper to render unto him those things which were his.
During the early days of Christianity people imagined
that Christ had come to be Caesar. They were disappointed when he refused, and finally killed him.

It is not uncommon for people in power to put
themselves in God's place. Some believe that all their
actions are the will of God. When a situation arises, as
in Rhodesia, some people confuse God with Caesar

and that they are acting in accordance with God's will even when it is obvious to everyone, including themselves, that for them to be Caesar or act in accordance with God's will, they must be legitimate. On 11 November 1965, Mr Smith declared unilateral independence in the name of God in the support of Western Christian civilization in Southern Africa. He believed he was halting Communism from spreading further down Africa beyond the Zambesi. In this case an illegitimate Caesar thought he was acting in accordance with God's will.

While I was detained at Sinoia Prison in 1971, criminals of all races were caned. Almost without exception they cried out pitifully calling to their mothers and God to help, and one wondered if people believed in God and in his help only when they are in difficulty. Those who were supposedly carrying out Caesar's instructions paid no attention to the people's calls to God. They went to church the following Sunday to confess their sins but carried on committing the same sins in want of a living. After one such beating the person carrying out the instructions said: 'God! Do you think this is God's prison? It is the white man's prison'; as if to imply that if the prisoner had cried out 'White man' the white men would have come to help him. In fact it was a white man who was inflicting the pain.

Another Sunday at the same prison, a member of the prison chaplaincy came to say Mass. When the prisoners had made their confessions, they received Holy Communion. Afterwards one of the prisoners said, 'I confessed all my sins including that of theft for which I am being imprisoned. And I was told that my sins were forgiven and received the body and blood of Our Lord. If I was good enough to do this and if my sins were forgiven, why then have I to continue being punished for this sin that has been forgiven?' Undoubtedly there was confusion in this person's mind between God and Caesar.

Theft is both a criminal offence and a sin. We understand that the sin is against God and the crime against the State. The offender is therefore answerable to two authorities, God and Caesar. God's forgiveness is instantaneous, but Caesar's may never come because once known to be a thief a person remains so all his life. But a person is one being and his actions can only be described as good or bad. Those services that we render to Caesar through our brotherhood are ultimately services to God.

There is a tendency among people to say that political matters are related to Caesar and religious matters are those that concern God. Every individual therefore would have to be a political or religious being—but never both at the same time. I do not agree with this way of thinking. Religion is only possible through our interaction with our fellow beings, and politics should not be separated from religion. Religion is a way of life which must have a bearing on our political life.

It is hypocritical to claim to be a Christian if the criminality of the Rhodesian way of life is overlooked. Black and white Christians should not kneel together before an altar receiving Holy Communion, pretending to be equal children of God, and to come out of that church and immediately accept separate development as a way of life. Where Caesar's laws interfere with the people's way of life, it is right that they should make a stand to stop that interference. The white priest who

believes that it is his duty to say Mass in an African
township and to receive higher wages than his African
counterpart might find refuge in the thought that he is
rendering unto Caesar the things that are Caesar's
because the situation in Rhodesia demands that of him.
The same priest might live in a white suburb or in a
comfortable house at a Mission station. He might justify
this on the grounds that he has been used to a higher
standard of living and that he can afford it. But is our
Christian brotherhood only relevant when it is of ad-
vantage to us? Or must we live and suffer for righteous-
ness as Christ did?

People like President Nyerere and President Kaunda
have suffered and yet retained their religious values.
They suffered for the sake of their people. As Christians
can they be asked not to take part in politics? Those
people in Rhodesia and beyond who hold strong
Christian values are often referred to as Communists by
the Rhodesian regime. In fact in recent statements,
leaders of the Rhodesian regime no longer refer to
Christianity when describing western civilisation, im-
plying that there is little difference between Christianity
and Communism. If Christians in Rhodesia had been
acting like good samaritans, the regime would find them
intolerable.

The Anglican Church in Rhodesia continues to raise
church levies from poor people in the rural areas, and
to identify itself with the illegal regime. It takes part
in the regime's commemorative services, but prevents
an African bishop of another denomination from reading
the Bible in the cathedral. The Church may allow white
politicians to meddle in its religion but it forbids black
political and religious leaders to take part in a religious
act. Black people in the Anglican Church are only made

suffragan bishops when they have no obvious political aspirations and agree to be stationed at centres which keep them out of sight.

An African woman, speaking to one of the Pearce Commissioners, said 'White Men came with the Bible and found us with the land, but now they have given us the Bible in exchange for the land.' Who would not say the same thing in Rhodesia today? Before the revolt of our people in 1896 the early missionaries used to live with the Africans and eat African food. After the revolt their attitude changed. In the Anglican church that same attitude continues to be the same even now under the illegal regime in Rhodesia. People like Bishop Skelton have been exceptional leaders in the Anglican Church. It did not surprise us when he had to leave the country. Also people like Bishop Lamont in the Roman Catholic Church are unique, not hesitating to condemn evil and to dissociate themselves from it. It may be argued that the stand Bishop Muzorewa is taking is in defence of his own rights, but these three Christian leaders have demonstrated true Christian humanity. It is impossible for human and thinking people to separate their lives into little compartments and label one compartment 'religious' and another 'political'; one 'white' and yet another 'black'. One cannot see one's friends suffering under the political evils of the illegal regime and stand aside, claiming that one's duty as a Christian is not to help but to look on. That kind of attitude is both cowardly and unChristian.

Three times I had to appear before the Rhodesian illegal 'Caesar' and on three occasions lengthy memoranda were submitted. At first I wished to refuse to appear before the Tribunal on the grounds that it was aiding the illegal regime and that its proceedings were

124

held in secret. But after careful consideration I wished to find out for myself, how much the regime knew of my activities. During the first hearing they accused me of aiding ZAPU members of the revolutionary movement. At a subsequent hearing they accused me of aiding ZANU members of the revolutionary movement. They required written representations before I appeared in person, which was done by my attorneys.

The first memorandum submitted to the Minister of Law and Order on 24 November 1970 as follows:

We have been instructed by Mr D.N.E. Mutasa to make the following objection and representations in respect of the Order for his detention which was deliviered to him on Wednesday 18th November 1970.

1. In the absence of any indication in the Detention Order as to your reasons for making it Mr Mutasa has had to make conjectures as to the reasons and as to the sort of information in your possession on which they may be based, and paragraphs 5, 6, 7 and 8 of this objection deal with specific matters which he thinks you may have had in mind. But he asks that in assessing any information in your possession you should take into account the general pattern of his conduct and intentions as outlined in paragraphs 2, 3 and 4.

2. Mr Mutasa was born in Rhodesia and is now 35 years of age. He grew up in a village development scheme on land at St Faith's Mission, Rusape where his father was a village headman, and he attended Goromonzi Secondary School. Later he joined the Federal Civil Service and worked as an administrative and executive officer in the Training Branch of the Department of Conservation and Extension. He supervised the Department's library and was in charge of the Information section. During the negotiations prior to the dissolution of the Federation he was twice sent to England by the Federal Civil Service Association as the only African member of the delegations negotiating conditions for civil servants after the dissolution. On his leaving the Federal Civil Service his senior officer paid tribute to his 'devotion to duty' and 'infectious enthusiams' and described him as

'thoroughly reliable'.

He was transferred to the Southern Rhodesian Civil Service, but at the age of 30 (then having a wife and three small children) he felt that he must get closer to the 'grass roots' in agricultural and community work, and resigned— giving up a salary at the rate of £85 per month—in order to do so.

Starting with a group of unemployed youths he then began the community development venture which has since developed as the Cold Comfort Farm Society, of which he has been Chairman up to the time of his detention.

About four years ago Mr Mutasa became a Director of the Nyafaru Development Company, having been asked to do so in order to help resolve difficulties which that organ- isation was facing.

Mr Mutasa is also a member of the National Council of the Red Cross Society of Rhodesia and an executive member of the Jiros Jiri Association and of the Salisbury Christian Action Group.

3. Mr Mutasa is aware that the Cold Comfort Farm Society is, or has been, regarded with suspicion in Government circles, but he draws your attention to what he belives to be (save for any over-generous reference to himself) a true and genuine view of that organisation and its aims and activities contained in the pamphlet annexed to this objection and marked 'A'.

4. Throughout his career Mr Mutasa's overriding concern has been the development of people, not only economically, helping them to make proper use of the land, but as human beings, helping them to live constructively and in harmony in a community. He accepts that politics cannot be divorced from life, but he is no militant politician. He has never been closely associated with any political party, and could never be regarded as in any sense a communist or communits- inclined except by the sort of person who would regard as such anyone trying to put the Christian gospel into practice. His approach has always been non-violent and non-racial. He is concerned with the welfare of white as well as black people, and in racial matters his influence has consistently been exerted in the direction of understanding and courtesy—

126

as he believes any Police or others having dealings with the Cold Comfort Farm Society would bear witness.

5. Judging by the timing of your Order for Mr Mutasa's detention it seems likely that what you had in mind was the resistance of the Tangwena people against being moved from land which they have previously occupied, and that you may believe Mr Mutasa's activities in the past have been in some way responsible for it and that, unless he is detained, his further activities in connection with the Tangwena may 'disturb or interfere with the maintenance of public order'.

In this connection Mr Mutasa emphatically affirms that nothing he has done in the past has gone beyond trying to interpret the views and feelings of some of the Tangwena people and helping them to avail themselves of legal assistance; and that nothing he would do if out of detention would go beyong this.

In doing what he has done the initiative has not come from him, and there has never been any question of his advising, let alone inciting, the Tangwena people to break the law. Some of them came to him, knowing him to be a person who was prepared to listen sympathetically and was capable in English and because he was connected with the occupiers of the neighbouring land, The Nyafaru Development Company; and Mr Mutasa believed that it was his duty, not only as a human being but as a citizen of the country, to try to understand their true feelings and to help in making them known, and to help them in obtaining whatever legal protection might be available to them; and he affirms that what he has done has been strictly confined to these activities.

However, Mr Mutasa thinks that information to a different effect may well have come into your hands. For example, there have been occasions when at a Court hearing the legal representatives of the accused have referred to Mr Mutasa for instructions, and he thinks it quite possible that persons preoccupied with the difficulty of the situation from the Government's point of view may have taken this as evidence that, instead of being wholly concerned as he was to interpret the wishes of the accused to their legal representatives, Mr Mutasa was encouraging them or even inciting them to break the law.

If this type of information is what you are relying on Mr Mutasa affirms that it is false, and he requests that you scrutinize carefully the possible motives and bias of those who may have supplied it.

6. Mr Mutasa points out that Rekayi Tangwena would have regarded it as entirely out of place for him (Mutasa), as a relatively young man and not even one of the Tangwena people, to have attempted to tell them, or even suggest to them, what they should do about the land; and that in talking to his people Rekayi Tangwena was at pains to make it clear to them that Mutasa was 'his boy', i.e. that his function was merely to act as an interpreter or messenger and not to give advice or make decisions. Mr Mutasa is in no doubt that Rekayi Tangwena would testify to this.

The only advice connected with the Tangwena which Mr Mutasa has been concerned with has been legal advice which he has passed on in his capacity as interpreter or go-between.

Mr Mutasa considers that it would be wholly mistaken to attribute the resistance of the Tangwena to promptings or incitement on his or anybody else's part.

7. It may be that you would consider even such activities in relation to the Tangwena as Mr Mutasa has confined himself to in the past would, if continued in the future, be likely to 'disturb or interfere with the maintenance of public order'. In that event Mr Mutasa submits that the appropriate action is not to disrupt his family life and other activities by detaining him in prison, but to revoke the detention order conditionally upon his refraining from further contact with the Tangwena people while the present situation subsists.

(We would mention that Mr Mutasa's first wife died and that he has married again and has a further young child of his second marriage).

8. The only other matters which Mr Mutasa can think of as possibly being connected with the issue of the Detention Order are his activities in the course of his recent visit overseas and his activities in connection with the 'African Peoples Association' presently in the process of being formed. He discounts the possibility of your regarding these activities as warranting his detention because, in the case of his visit

overseas, nothing arising from it would be classifiable as acts
'in Rhodesia' which would endanger the public safety as
mentioned in the Order, and in the case of the African Peoples
Association, if you considered it a threat to the maintenance
of public order, it would have been open to you to act under
the Unlawful Organisations Act. However, Mr Mutasa would
like to make it clear—

(a) That as regards his visit overseas there was nothing clan-
destine or subversive about it, and that in all he had to say
he did his utmost to be truthful and objective.

(b) That as regards the African Peoples Association, the
objects in its draft Constitution are as follows:

'To promote unity, understanding, friendship, co-operation
and development among people, by research into the conditions necessary to establish good human relationships;
by the education of members and others in high personal
standards of conduct and in social responsibility and
service; by helping in the solution of social and economic
problems both local and national; by encouraging the
growth of constructive political, economic, educational
and social activities, and by participating in any activity
contributing to the progress of the people of Rhodesia.'

And so far as Mr Mutasa is concerned there are no ulterior
objects.

8. If the Detention Order arises from any other activity of
or information about Mr Mutasa he asks to be given an
indication of what it is, so that he may make further representations.

9. Mr Mutasa sincerely believes in the principle of partnership, and that the kind of objectives he has tried to achieve
in the course of his activities are in the best interests of
people as a whole in Rhodesia, whether black or white; and
in particular, as regards his activities in connection with the
Tangwena, that it is in the best interests of white people
that they should have direct and not merely second-hand
knowledge of how the Tangwena people feel. And he submits that to condemn to detention someone who is concerned to bring about mutual understanding is not in the
best interests even of the white people.

10. Mr Mutasa asks that the Detention Order be revoked

forthwith

Dated at Salisbury this 24th day of November 1970.

SCANLEN & HOLDERNESS,
Objector's Attorneys.

The Review Tribunal met and considered this lengthy memorandum. I gave evidence on oath and was cross-examined. On that occasion too, argument was submitted by my attorney, Mr Anthony Eastwood.

All matters which were revealed to us were commented upon. However the Chairman of the Tribunal announced that certain information which was in fact the basis for my continued detention had not been revealed.

We wrote again in September 1971 to Mr Wrangle at the Secretary for Law and Order's Office stressing that I had 'at no time acted as an adviser to Chief Tangwena'; that I did not have a 'hate for Europeans' as my numerous contacts with Europeans proved;, that there was nothing sinister in my discussions with visiting British members of Parliament; that the Christian Action Group of which I was chairman until 1967—1969, was in no way subversive (on occassions speakers included members of the Government party); that I first learned of the association with ZAPU of Mr Hassan whom I met at Cold Comfort Farm, from the Tribunal at the last hearing; that whilst I sympathised with and attended some student protest meetings at the University, it was a 'smear and a lie' to say that I attempted to recruit any students to engage in espionage; that although the Cold Comfort Farm Society was aware after 1968 (following a statement in Parliament by the Minister of Internal Affairs) that it could expect to be banned at some time, no attempt to obstruct such a banning was ever offered.

We also pointed to the peaceful and reconciling aims of the Cold Comfort Farm Society and its concern for the wider problems of the consequences of industrialisation and human relationships. Finally I undertook that if released I would be prepared to leave Rhodesia or to be restricted to my land in the area of St Faiths. (Which is government property and not Tribal Trust Land.)

Again the appeal was unsuccessful. However, the third and final memorandum from my attorneys, submitted on 15 June 1972, shows how the regime could act when it chose to.

On the 14th June, 1972, we received a letter from Mr Mutasa, dated the 10th June, enclosing your letter dated 2nd June advising of the proposed review on the 19th June, and enclosing a copy of the representations forwarded to you by Mr Mutasa.

Mr Mutasa has requested us to produce certain witnesses to the Tribunal, but it will take some little time to trace these witnesses, interview them and prepare for the hearing. It will not be possible to do all this by the 19th June. We confirm that our Mr Shaw spoke to you on the telephone today in this regard and you informed him that there would be no postponement of the review. In our respectful submission the short notice given of the present review amounts to a denial of the due process of the review as there will be insufficient time to prepare and present the evidence of the witnesses Mr Mutasa wishes to call. As there are no rules applicable to an application for a postponement and no appeal, we can only ask that the Chairman of the Tribunal give such directions as he considers appropriate in the circumstances.

The witnesses referred to above relate to an incident which was raised on the first occasion that Mr Mutasa appeared before the Tribunal. At the time the identity of the person with whom Mr Mutasa was alleged to have had subversive dealings was not revealed to him. Subsequently in October, 1971, Inspector Pay visited Mr Mutasa at

Sinoia Prison and informed him of the identity of this person. It is this person Mr Mutasa now wishes to call as a witness.

As regards the remaining aspects of Mr Mutasa's case, we have nothing to add (save in one respect) to the representations submitted at the first hearing and in our letter of the 21st September, 1971. We would ask the Tribunal to consider afresh the contents of that letter. We would again re-iterate that Mr Mutasa would like the opportunity to reply on any information which the Tribunal is now prepared to reveal to him but has not in the past been prepared to do. It appears that in view of the passing of the years there may well be occasion to reveal such information.

The one aspect to which we do draw further attention concerns Mr Mutasa's release on licence to take up studies in the United Kingdom. Enquiries are in hand as to making the necessary arrangements. The Tribunal is asked earnestly to consider recommending Mr Mutasa's release from Salisbury Prison on the following terms:

(a) Mr Mutasa obtained satisfactory evidence of his acceptance at an educational institution in the United Kingdom, and of his financial means to take up such education.
(b) He leave forthwith for the United Kingdom;
(c) He refrain from all unlawful activity;
(d) Other usual conditions.

On the 25th July 1972 my attorneys wrote to me:

Dear Didymus,

Following our conference on the 23rd July I have a number of matters to report. HEKS has granted a scholarship for you of Swiss Fracs 700 monthly for a two-year period in Great Britain or another English-speaking country plus travelling expenses from Rhodesia to the country of study. HEKS further advises that a specific plan at improving your knowledge of farming is under preparation. I have had no reply from the Special Branch following upon my enquiries to them as to the whereabouts of Mr amd Mrs Kalowa. I have explained the circumstances to the Secretary for Law and Order who is also the Secretary of the review tribunal. I again interviewed Gertrude as regards her recollection of any visit by Mr or Mrs Kalowa or both. Without

132

actually seeing that person she has no recollection of them.
I have now been informed that it is now proposed to hear
the review of your detention by the Review Tribunal on the
15 August 1972 at 9 a.m. at Salisbury Prison. This will
shortly be confirmed and I will keep you informed of developments. It will be necessary for me to interview you before the
hearing and this I will do probably in about the first week of
August. The question of your marriage is being taken up, as
you know, by Mr Tanser on your behalf. I hope to have
something further to report in this regard shortly.

Best wishes,

Yours sincerely,

Scanlen & Holderness.

During the course of the hearings referred to above,
it became quite obvious to me how ill-informed the
illegal regime is of what goes on in the country. Its
interference in one's private life is an example of what
happens to the lives of 5½ million people in Rhodesia.
Thousands of them are going through the same prison
experiences as mine. The control of our religious and
political institutions is still in the hands of white
people. We wish to determine our own lives and to
change completely the present pattern of life which is
imposed on us. It is inevitable that this change will
come, and obvious that it may not be a peaceful change.
This is not the fault of Africans. The Rhodesian 'God'
and 'Caesar' is symbolized by the white men's desire
to uproot everything of value to us and replace it with
their own version of western standards. Our black
leaders realise this and they do not want these 'standards'
to be imposed on their people.

The legal representations must have helped, because
on 27 November 1972, the regime decided to let me
leave my place of detention but without withdrawing
the detention order. This is shown by a letter dated

10 October 1973 I received in Brimingham from Mr A.G. Eccles of the Secretary for Law and Order's office which reads:

Dear Sir,

The Review Tribunal, established in terms of section 27 of the Emergency Powers (Maintenance of Law and Order) Regulations, 1973, is required to review every detention order in terms of the said regulations.

The Tribunal has informed me that it is proposed to review the order against you on or about 13th November, 1973 and I am directed to enquire whether you wish to make representations in writing for consideration by the Tribunal.

Should you wish to make any such representations notice should be submitted to the Secretary, Review Tribunal, Private Bag 7703, Causeway, Salisbury, Rhodesia on or before 31st October, 1973.

Yours faithfully,

A.G. ECCLES
for Secretary for Law and Order

How frightened can a regime be which finds it necessary to detain a person who is out of the country?

10
Out of Prison

Up to the time of my detention I had visited prison on many occasions. On average, we made a trip to Gwelo every three months with Stella Nadzimbamuto, Esnath Musarurwa and Charlotte Msipa when their husbands were detained in Gwelo Prison. These trips were more or less social occasions; sometimes taking the children to see their fathers. We started the three hours' journey at 6 a.m. to be there at 9 a.m. If we were lucky our visits took place and were over by 11.30 a.m., before the hard labour prisoners came into feed. Sometimes we had to go back after 2 p.m. All visits had to be over by 3 p.m. We had three hours' journey back home where we arrived by 7 p.m. at the latest. So we walked out of prison and just went home, with at times the odd disappointed wife to pacify.

At first visiting the detainees was just a charitable action but then the case of Daniel Madzimbamato made me feel that there was more to it. He was offered an opportunity to leave Rhodesia but could only leave his country as a free man. I must have walked out of prison more than twenty times and observed the opening and the closing of the enormous doors without realising its effect on those remaining behind. Those visits were a symbol of solidarity with my friends, at the end of which arrangements for the next visit had to be made—perhaps to deliver a bag of sugar, a shirt or a writing pad.

But on 27 November 1972, everything was quite different. I had waited a long time in suspense, but there had been indications that I might be released on 16 October, 1972. My mother, who was coming to see me more often during this period, had whispered that the illegal regime had issued a passport for me and my family. But when this date came no word was said about my release. My lawyer was due to see me that afternoon. He did not come. Gertrude, her parents, my mother and brothers had come to our marriage that morning; but as we were not allowed to discuss anything, they left me with the impression that I might be released that afternoon and allowed to go to Epworth Mission where Gertrude and the children were living.

Once we were locked up Enos Nkala, Robert Mugabe, Maurice Nyagumba, Morton Malianga, Edgar Tekere and I began to guess at the reasons why nothing had happened, but we heard nothing until the following Monday when Gertrude was permitted to visit us. She brought with her an application form for a British passport and the information that we could not be allowed into Britain on a Rhodesian passport. And that we had to apply for an entry permit. British laws could not be bent, least of all for the wretched on the earth. With great speed we obtained both of these by 31 October, 1972. When the passport got to Salisbury, we then discovered that the illegal regime would not let us travel on a British passport.

Towards the end of 1970, Farai Madzimbamuto had his British passport confiscated and he was stopped from travelling to attend school in England. His mother was called into the Immigration Office to be informed. When we asked the immigration official why he was finding it pleasant to jeopardise this young man's educational future he said 'Farai is not a British citizen; so I cannot allow him to travel on a British passport.' We asked him whether, being white, he, as a Rhodesian civil servant had one. 'Yes', he said 'You see, you cannot compare him with me. He was born here.' This was quite right. But Farai was born in Rhodesia. If he had been white, he would have been entitled to a British passport, just as other white people born in Rhodesia. The question of his right to have a British passport would not have arisen.

It looked as if our right to use one was questioned by the illegal regime. Bishop Muzarewa and Rev. Canaan Banana had had their passports confiscated. There was little hope that we would be treated differently. It took about three weeks, however, for our lawyers to clear the matter up.

On Friday, 24 November, 1972, the following message was sent to me by Mr Ruff, the officer-in-charge, Salisbury Prison. 'To Detainee Mutasa. Reference you release. You fly on Monday. Congratulations.' I spent the weekend discussing the future with my colleagues and taking advice from them.

Lawyers had looked into the whole question of my detention and their view had been that unless I had specific complaints about conditions, the courts in Rhodesia would not hear my case, particularly if it challenged the regime's right or authority to detain me. Lawyers had advised that the British Government was answerable for my detention but it would not be brought to court in Rhodesia, where no law or authority was recognised by the British Government. So during the last weekend of my detention, colleagues advised me to take legal proceedings against the British Government.

Our concern is to have all the issues clarified. We wish to examine every legal aspect of the Rhodesian problem. We want to be able to say we knocked at every door and followed every course in our search for freedom. This will be of immense value to those who may wish to continue the struggle. It will help them to make up their minds to follow only those ways which appear hopeful to them. We must, in the end, convince ourselves that there is only one way to freedom. Can the liberal approach bear any fruitful solutions to the fascist behaviour of the white minority government? If and when it has been shown that it does not bear fruit, then other methods of finding a solution will have to be applied. Only when their way has been fully exhausted will liberals conform.

After all these discussions during the weekend—at last Monday came. There was no indication of when the flight might be. I still hoped that I might be released some time before the flight, and be given the chance to see my friends and to say goodbye. A colleague, Solomon Wekwete, was given some days to travel to his home to see his parents before his departure. When the door of the cell opened, I hoped the same was going to apply to me. Instead I was told that there were visitors to see me. These were my two brothers, John and Cyprian, and my mother. It was obvious that my release would be different from that of Solomon and would be more like that of Matthew Malowa. During the visit I learnt that all the travelling documents were ready, and that many friends had come from Inyanga, St Faiths and Enkeldoorn to see us off.

Afterwards I was escorted back to the cell. Edgar and I played our last game of Tsoro and I lost a set of three games. He was pleased that he won and so was I. We were playing a game with definite rules. Maurice Nyagumbo watched and sometimes took part. He was keen and wanted me to win. There also was Enos Nkala, Robert Mugabe, who knew the game better than us, and Morton Malianga. All these friends were on my side, not because I was going away but they knew that Edgar was better at the game than I was. They were following the principle that the weakest should be protected, a strong and good principle of our culture. Other cultures emphasise the exploitation of the weak and describe ours as primitive. Those who have sought to understand our cultural values must have discovered how beautiful they are—simple and straightforward.

At lock up, when my belongings had been removed, Robert Mugabe was exercising while he was taking a shower. The picture of him hopping in the shower is still vivid in my memory. And so are the words 'Wa Mutasa mufambe zwakanake, ('Mutasa, travel safe'). They said in unision with voices half-raised: 'Don't forget the struggle.' No one would. But when the enormous doors had closed behind me, the words we had just been speaking became memories. The picture of the people I had been seeing was now only imaginery. The formulation of our group's history I suppose.

Going down the steps, from the top floor of our block, I realised that I was probably going down the steps for the last time. I remembered the first day I went up the steps, carrying my belongings and observing all the features of the block. This time the steps were leading me to the outside world. A free world?

Time will tell.

In the superintendent's office, Mr B.A. Ruff, the officer-in-charge, looked very much like the head-master of my previous secondary school. He produced a bundle of letters that he had withheld and asked me to see if there were any that were missing. He express-ed pleasure that I was leaving. In a sense, the pleasure was sincere. Looking after detainees can be a hard task. One does not know exactly how to behave. In our Rhodesian situation, Mr Ruff was aware that he could be given orders by any one of the detainees he was holding. His manner had to be courteous. He tried to do this when he could and got told off when he did not. 'Goodbye,' he said, 'you will be fetched at 6.30 p.m.' It was obvious that he was not going to say by whom—so I did not ask.

I went to sit down on a bench at the entrance of the prison and talked to an African warder who was letting people in and out. These were prisoners. He asked after the lives of detainees 'Who are there at present?' he asked 'What are their names?'

I looked through the pages of *Kontakion For You Departed* by Alan Paton, which had been sent to me by Jack and Ida Grant. This had been withheld. Then there was a heavy knock at the gate. Two people came in. One came up to me and asked if I was Mutasa. The other went to sign a book. The first one explained that they had come to take me to the airport, where my family would be. He said I should behave myself on the way and wilfully displayed a revolver.

Carrying a carton of books in one hand and a suit-case of clothes in the other, I followed the two men to a Volkswagen parked at the entrance and took the back seat. Driving along Enterprise Road and looking at Salisbury Prison, it made a different impression from my frevious one, when I was going in and out of it. I knew the place this time. It was no longer just a prison but a place where I had lived and through which my personal experience is reflected. Driving along Jameson Avenue towards the centre of Salisbury, memories came of the countless times that I had driven along that road travelling between Inyanga and Cold Comfort Farm. Some parts were changing. An enormous building was under construction in Salisbury Gardens. The C.I.D. told me it was a new hotel. This was for the affluent society—another place which might bear the sign 'Whites only. Right of admission reserved'.

Along Kingsway, the C.I.D. became communicative. They asked questions. 'What are you going to study?' 'Will you go to see your Swiss friends?' 'Will you behave yourself?' To the last question they received a polite answer that as the father of four I could not misbehave. I made it clear, of course, that I shall continue to be one with all our people and to do whatever they require of me.

'Are you going to continue to take part in politics?'

'There are little Rhodesian politics in Britain. But I cannot see myself doing nothing about it.'

'Do you want to return to this country?'

'Yes. This is my country.'

'I hope you will let us know when you intend to return.'

We had travelled past the Cranborne Army Barracks and were going towards the airport. They had had answers to the questions which were important in their minds—so they changed the subject and talked about beer. They criticised the English beer as tasteless and asked what I would drink. After a couple of years without beer I did not think I would drink it again. But for the sake of identity with the Irish, I said Guinness.

At this point the conversation stopped and my thoughts turned to consider where the two young white men were born. Without asking them I was certain that they had been born in Britain. And now they were engaged in keeping the indigenous people of Rhodesia down.

We arrived at Salisbury Airport at 7 p.m. and entered through a side entrance which led to the immigration offices. I sat on my carton of books in the hall, and waited for the arrival of my family. One of the men came regularly to see if I was still there. At 7.30 p.m. I asked if it was possible to say goodbye to my relatives who I thought had arrived. He went away to find out and brought the answer that I could see them for three minutes. He led the way into the visitors lounge and one of Gertrude's friends came forward to greet me. We took a seat and were told to speak in English. After a short while most people who were outside came in. Within a short time there was a crowd and the police whisked me from them immediately. We stayed for ten minutes in the lounge, thanks to my mother's late arrivel. Arthur Chadzengwa managed to whisper that Peter Nieswand had failed to come to the airport because the police were questioning him.

It is surprising that Judith Todd and Peter Nieswand, those young white Rhodesians who opposed the regime, were born and brought up in Rhodesia. Maybe they are opposed to Afrikaner domination. The Afrikaner had originally only been noticeable in agriculture and in the Rhodesian Ministry of Works. Now their presence is felt in almost every sphere of Rhodesian life, the civil service and private business.

Gertrude had managed to press her way through the crowd to tell me that she and the children had arrived and was having our luggage weighed. As we went to the departure lounge the crowd of friends walked up the stairs to the balcony. As they were waiting there, the Rhodesian Security Police had the pleasure of serving on me the third order from the illegal regime. A permit to leave Rhodesia which read as follows:

I wish I could remember the names of the two Rhodesian Security Police Officers who served this notice 'on or to the withinmentioned person by handing it to him personally at Salisbury Airport'. I cannot read their signatures, so perhaps they do not wish to be remembered.

I am not surprised that the regime continued my detention order and that according to the Permit I can only travel in my country under police escort. Indeed the regime is still considering the review of my detention order.

When the terms of the permit had been explained to me, Gertrude and the children came into the depature lounge. The security policemen stood at the door and watched us walking towards the South African Airways jumbo jet. We stopped to wave to our friends at the balcony. The two policemen beckoned us to walk on. One of our friends said, 'don't forget us?' I will never forget as long as I live and continue to identify myself with my fellow men. It is impossible to forget.

Postscript

On arrival in England life's duties did not seem to leave me a moment to rest. There were arrangements to be made in London about my year's study at Fircroft College, friends to see in London, and the journey to Birmingham where we had never been before.

At Heathrow Airport Mrs Eleanor Jaffey and Mr Leslie Jenkins of Exeter Amnesty International welcomed us to England and gave us warm clothes. This was a most desirable gesture of friendship. Mrs Jaffey lived in Rhodesia and worked for the welfare of detainees in Rhodesia. It was very pleasant to notice that she was working harder here and had other people interested in looking after my family during the period of my detention. Mr Jenkins is the chairman of the Exeter Group of Amnesty International, which continues to be interested in our welfare in this country.

As well as Mr Jenkins and Mrs Jaffery we were also met by an official of the British Council and given details of my grant to study at Fircroft College.

Time passed very quickly and soon we were on the train to Birminham. As we sped northwards it was interesting to listen to the children's first comments about this country. Edwin started by saying, 'White people here work for themselves. Did you notice those digging a trench as we drove from Heathrow?' Euphemia confirmed, 'The taxi driver was a white man.' They had travelled by taxi from the Headquarters of Amnesty International to Euston Station whilst I had gone to the office of the British Council. Martin then said, 'Can't you see white people in this coach. This does not happen in Rhodesia.' The conversation went on in Shona. People sitting next to us would have been greatly surprised by it.

On arrival at New Street Station, Birmingham, we exhibited our Rhodesian ignorance. We had been told that we would be met at the station in Birmingham. So we stayed on the platform hoping that our host would come there. She, Mrs Irene Corfield, wife of the Principal of Fircroft College, was waiting for us up the stairs in the station hall. Finally she came to find us on the platform and took us home. I gather that we were not the only ones caught up in this new situation. Someone from a foreign country was told that he would be met at Liverpool Station in London. On arrival in London he took the train to Liverpool city and waited at the station. In the meantime his host had lost patience and gone back home. The guest 'phoned the host at home, and told the host that he was miles away from London!

Mrs Corfield fed us well, and then took us to Mr and Mrs Leigh's home at 213 Pershore Road where we lived up to the end of April 1973. The Leigh's family was good and gave us our first briefing about life in this country. Mr and Mrs Leigh are black people and come from West Africa, he from Sierra Leone and she from Nigeria.

On 29th November 1972, a day after we arrived in this country, Guy and Molly Clutton-Brock came to meet us. We immediately felt as if we were at Cold

Comfort Farm again. We went to the Bull Ring Centre to buy pots and pans and blankets for our household.

Fircroft College served a very good purpose. There was a cross-section of people from nearly all walks of life. The educational system was very good for me. The sessions when 'student papers' were presented were the most educative. Every Monday morning and Friday evening a student read a paper on a subject of his choice. The range of subjects chosen and read was very wide. During the discussion which followed every reading of a paper was also very interesting. It was here that it was obvious that human suffering and anxiety is everywhere. 'You talk of the working class as if you have never seen one. What do you feel about the way they live? I must tell you that it is not very nice to eat bread and drink water every day. Some of us have tasted butter for the first time at this College, and that is what Liberal Democracy means to us.'

It was necessary to make arrangements to comply with the wishes of my colleagues at Salisbury Prison as soon as possible. Varying advice was given to me by many friends. There was need to communicate with them from time to time but this was stopped by the Salisbury regime.

Following advice carefully, we finally arrived at the point where the opinions referred to below were given. A problem of finance arose so it was necessary to go to Switzerland to see friends. At the same time I took the opportunity to talk with people about our problem. Then it was necessary to go to Sweden and meet people there.

During these travels my impression of how people regard the Rhodesian problem was that everyone puts the blame on Mr Smith. Even those people who help

147

him. When they realised that my view was not the same as theirs, and that I regard it mainly as a failure by white people, their attitude changed. Some admitted this failure and others defended themselves.

On arriving in Britain, I had sought help from various organizations in bringing a case against the British Government for neglecting its responsibilities towards me. After several fruitless requests for legal aid, the International Defence and Aid Fund agreed to meet the cost of obtaining a Legal Opinion from a distinguished barrister, Mr Anthony Lester.

He advised that in a previous case, the Crown produced a certificate 'to the effect that the alleged liability of the Crown arose otherwise than in respect of Her Majesty's Government in the United Kingdom' which effectively blocked any action in the English courts. The Southern Rhodesia Act, 1965, and the Order-in-Council which accompanied it transferred the power to make laws back to Her Majesty's Council and made it 'clear beyond doubt that the United Kingdom Parliament has resumed full power to legislate for Rhodesia and has removed from Rhodesia the power to legislate for itself'. But the British Government had not necessarily accepted *liability* for acts in Rhodesia as though they had taken place in part of the United Kingdom. Mr Lester also advised that an appeal to the Court of Human Rights under the European Convention for the Protection of Human Rights and Fundamental Freedoms, 1950, would be bound to fail since 'at no time has the British Government extended the Convention to Southern Rhodesia' specifically, as it would be required to, under Article 63.

A number of people who saw the Opinion and discussed it with me, felt that I was in the position of the